
PERGAMON PROGRAMMED TEXTS

General Editor: F. H. GEORGE

produced in association with Teaching Programmes Limited

An Introduction to Digital Computing

CERTIFICATE OF VALIDATION

The results in validating this text
will be found on page vi

PERGAMON PROGRAMMED TEXTS

An Introduction to
Digital Computing

by

F. H. GEORGE
M.A., Ph.D., F.R.S.S.
University of Bristol

PERGAMON PRESS
OXFORD · LONDON · EDINBURGH · NEW YORK
TORONTO · PARIS · BRAUNSCHWEIG

Pergamon Press Ltd., Headington Hill Hall, Oxford
4 & 5 Fitzroy Square, London W.1

Pergamon Press (Scotland) Ltd., 2 & 3 Teviot Place, Edinburgh 1

Pergamon Press Inc., 44–01 21st Street, Long Island City, New York 11101

Pergamon of Canada, Ltd., 6 Adelaide Street East, Toronto, Ontario

Pergamon Press S.A.R.L., 24 nie des Écoles, Paris 5e

Friedr. Vieweg & Sohn Verlag, Postfach 185, 33 Braunschweig, West Germany

---

First edition 1966
Library of Congress Catalog Card No. 65-27375

Printed in Great Britain by Billing & Sons Limited, Guildford and London

(2515/66)

Contents

VALIDATION CERTIFICATE

THIRTY selected subjects worked through the programme. These ranged from Science students at University, Art students at an Art College, Science Sixth Formers at a Grammar School and lay executives including a T.V. Producer. Their ages ranged between 18 years and 39 years.

A Pre-test was given to the students before reading the programme to establish the amount of subject matter, contained in the programme, which they already knew.

Whilst working through the programme the students recorded their answers on the standard response sheets supplied.

When the students had completed the programme a Post-test was given, which in this case was different from the Pre-test. Due to this fact it was not possible to obtain a measurable gain in knowledge, but it is possible to see an increase in understanding by noting the difference between the average Pre-test and Post-test scores.

The average time taken to read the programme was 6½ hours.

Results

Pre-test:	Maximum Score	15%
	Minimum Score	6%
	Average Score	10.9%
Post-test:	Maximum Score	93%
	Minimum Score	67%
	Average Score	82.4%

Editor's Preface

THIS new series of Programmed Books represents a major step towards the universal availability of programmed material. It is hoped ultimately to supply books for every subject that human beings may wish to learn.

The text of these programmed books is not arranged in the sequence to which we are accustomed in ordinary books. The reader follows *the routing directions on each page*, so that in the *branching* type of programme he will simply select, from among the alternatives offered to him at the foot of the frame, the number of the frame which he believes contains the right answer. This method has been evolved because it has great advantages, from the instructional point of view, over the usual page-to-page sequence, and it will very soon be found to be equally easy to follow.

In the *linear* programme, the reader will generally proceed in the usual way to the frame on the immediately following page, unless he is specifically told to turn to some other frame.

The programmes are written in a manner which gives the reader the maximum clarity of exposition. He is taken through the subject step by step, and each step is reinforced with a question which must be answered correctly before he can proceed to the next step.

In addition to its value as an instructional work, each programmed text is followed by an index; this not only enables the reader to refer to definitions of vital terms, but also serves the purpose of a reference book.

It is intended that this new library of programmed books will gradually accumulate texts in every subject, including science, the arts, engineering, mathematics, specialized topics such as digital computers, as well as subjects with the broad sweep of architecture and planning.

With the development of a large number of such programmed books, it is planned to supply programmed texts that will themselves offer integrating material, and such titles as *Philosophy of Science* and *Dynamic Planning* will appear in due course. These texts will be closely associated with guide books that can route the student through the sets of various texts, in pursuit of some particular goal. This can be done in much the same way as a student is routed through a single text.

A student wishing to achieve, say, A-level in three subjects, will be able to find, in the near future, the set of programmed books that he needs to carry him to the required standard; though a person who wants to understand some new branch of engineering, for example, may have to select his books carefully, to compile precisely the information he requires.

It is because this library hopes to satisfy people with vastly differing needs that each volume will be autonomous. Each subject may be repeated in more than one text to give instruction appropriate to different sorts of requirements, such as different age groups, and research is being carried out on the possibility of catering for other individual differences.

It may be that the linear form of programming is more suitable for some subjects, and branching programmes more suitable for others. We shall, however, provide texts in both forms whenever there is a good case for so doing.

The first batch of programmed books—due to arrive on the market in 1966—contains texts on mathematics, science and computers, as well as topics of general interest. These will be followed by many more programmed books written at every level of complexity, for our scope is no less than the educational needs of the community as a whole. We are confident that they will have a wide appeal, and consequently they will be presented in a flexiback binding that is economical to produce, as well as being highly durable.

An important feature of these books is that they are all carefully checked and validated. This means that each text will have been read through by a number of experienced programmers, and tried out on a sample of the people for whom the book is intended. A statement to this effect, as well as a note as to what has been assumed about the reader's background, will be found in the Author's Preface.

It is considered that this series represents a major advance in publishing, in that it will gradually accumulate information, properly prepared in a specialized way, that may well revolutionize teaching facilities, both in this country and overseas.

In conclusion, we offer a word of warning. For the same reasons that it is impossible to achieve agreement among teachers as to the best approach to any particular subject, we do not expect that all our texts, however good, will meet with universal approval. Readers are individuals, with varying backgrounds and often with special needs, and this is why we must have many different treatments of the same subject in the field of programmed instruction.

F. H. GEORGE

Author's Preface

THIS programme has been written for the person with a scientific and mathematical type of interest. It is, in fact, intended for the interested layman or that almost mythical person, called by Virginia Woolf, the Common Reader, but it is a common reader with a definite bias towards numbers. The text contains multiple choice questions and direct questions and you should think carefully about the answer to every question before you go on to the next frame. If you wish to make a game of it, count 2 points for every direct question and 4 points for every indirect question answered correctly first time; 2 points if you are correct second time, provided of course there are at least three alternatives. Then keep a tally of all the points you obtain.

This programme is written in such a way that it should be possible to understand the text without any prior knowledge of computers. However, it does make a few assumptions of knowledge, especially of elementary arithmetic. It also assumes that you will not become faint-hearted if symbols like x, y and z are used from time to time.

This programme has been read and checked by eight specialists in computers. It has been validated on university students who have had no previous knowledge of computers, as well as on a small number of ordinary adults. Resulting from the validation tests, many questions were added, and the programme has been reconstructed several times.

The author wishes to express his gratitude for help received in reading, advising, testing and validating this programme to Scientific Systems Limited, Teaching Programmes Limited, as well as Mr. O. B. Chedzoy, Computer Section, Bristol College of Advanced Technology; Dr. M. J. Apter, Educational and Scientific Developments Ltd., Bristol; Mr. Richard Goodman, Department of Cybernetics, Brighton College of Advanced

Technology; Mr. Dennis Boston, Computer Section, Bristol Siddeley Engines Ltd; and Dr. M. H. Rogers, Department of Mathematics, University of Bristol.

It is recognized that this field is changing quickly and that by now a new generation of computers has become available. They are, however, still based on the same principles outlined in this programme.

F. H. GEORGE

To the Reader

In this book the material does not generally follow serially in the usual way; furthermore each page may contain more than one block of information, or frames as we call them.

Each frame contains several numbers. In the top outside corner is the frame number itself: in the top left hand corner is a number showing the frame which the reader has just left.

At the bottom of each frame are instructions for reaching the next frame. These may be simply:

Turn to **256.**

Alternatively the reader may be given a number of different frames to choose from, where the actual choice depends upon his answer to the question on that frame.

The reader should also have paper or a notebook for making notes or doing calculations. To obtain maximum benefit from the programme, calculations should be done before the answer is looked up, and the instructions given should be obeyed.

CHAPTER ONE

The Organization of a Computer

IN THIS first chapter on Digital Computing, we outline the basic workings of the computer, including the way it handles simple arithmetical problems.

This first chapter serves as a brief general survey of the principal features of a typical computer. We can say that a typical computer divides into three sections:

(1) The input and output system.
(2) The memory system for storage of data.
(3) A processing system, including calculating units and control units for interpreting and following the stored programme.

Turn to **2**

from 1

This course is an introduction to digital computing, and it is our intention to explain it to you, assuming that this is the first time you have studied it, and we shall take you through to the point where, with a minimum of instruction *on a particular machine*, you should be able to carry out computations for yourself.

There are many different makes of digital computer, so you would have to get to know each make separately, but this should be easy, once you understand the general principles on which all digital computers work.

Turn to **3**

from 2

Now, as you know, we shall often ask questions during the course of this programme, and these will usually be based on what you have just read. So let us start by telling you a few simple facts about computers.

Digital computers are much like arithmeticians; they have, inside them, *stores* (which we can say are made up of *registers*) and electronic *arithmetic units* (which include *adders*, *subtractors*, and the like). So that if we send two numbers (let us call them x and y) from the store to the adder together, we shall receive back their sum $x + y$.

So if we send the message "subtract 10 from 12" to the arithmetic unit, what shall we receive back?

Think of the answer and turn to **4**

4

from 3

If we subtract 10 from 12, we get back 2 from the arithmetic unit.

Suppose we sent 3 and 4 from the store to the adder, and when we got back the sum, we sent it with 8 to the subtractor, where we do the subtracting *from* 8.

What is the result?

7. 1.
12. -1.
14. 0.

Go to the frame (**7**, **12** or **14**) which you think is opposite the correct answer.

5

from 7

-4 is your answer.

But $A - B$ is $A(8) - B(4)$, i.e. $8 - 4$, and this is not equal to -4.

Return to **7** and choose another answer

from 13

The register with address *A* contains 8.
Look again at our diagram, this time with the registers empty:

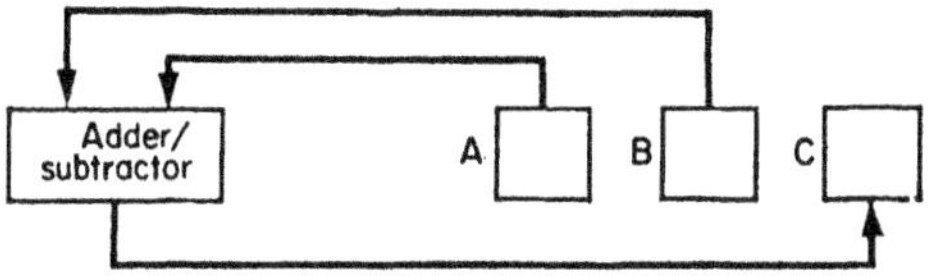

Each register (A, B or C) can send a number into the adder, and the answer could go back to either A, B or C.

This is done by the *control* selecting the addresses from which the numbers are to be taken to operate on. Now it is the job of the *programmer*, the man who *organizes* the flow of information in the computer (the set of instructions is the programme), to ensure the correct operation of the computer.

e.g. Take numbers from *A* and *B* and send *to* the *adder*.
Take the sum *from* the *adder* and put it in *C*.

Suppose we send 4 and 3 into the arithmetic unit, what would we get back?

Turn to **8**

7

from 4

1 is correct. $3 + 4 = 7$ and $8 - 7 = 1$. The adder and the subtractor work in turn on the numbers.

Look at the following diagrammatic representation of the adding part of the process:

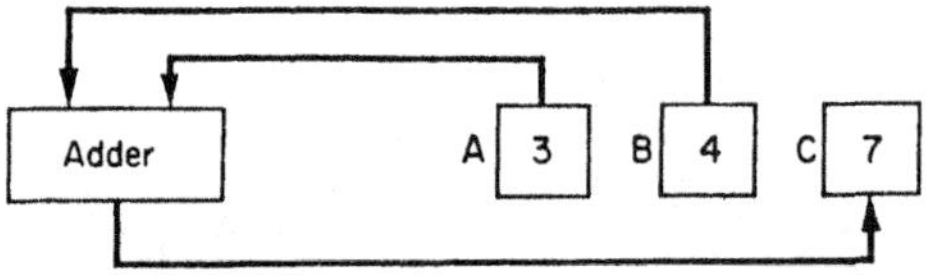

Register *A* (the registers, remember, make up the store) supplies 3, *B* supplies 4 and *C* gets the answer 7.

Suppose *A* supplied 8 and *B* supplied 4, and we had a subtractor instead of an adder. If the contents of *B* were subtracted from *A* and the answer placed in *C*, what would *C* finally contain?

5. -4.
11. 4.
17. 12.

from 6

It depends on the instruction. If it were ADD, we would get 7 back, if SUBTRACT then 1 or − 1, and so on.

Now we must tell you that to get the best out of this course on computers you should have a notebook, pencil and rubber and be prepared to work out examples.

You will often be asked to work out sums ("problems" or "computations" mean the same thing), and so, without paper and pencil, at the very least, you can hardly hope to get the best from this programme.

Now note that a computer must be able to store *instructions* and *numbers*. These are fed in at the beginning of the computer operation, and stored in registers until they are needed. The instructions, of course, are the operations or functions such as add, subtract, etc., which operate on the numbers.

How do we identify any particular register?

Turn to **9**

from 8

We can identify any register by its *address*.

We have said that a computer must be able to store *numbers*, and also *instructions* by which the computer operates on the numbers, and the principal purpose is to send numbers to our arithmetic unit, to have them added, subtracted, divided, etc.

Both numbers and instructions are stored in what we call *registers*, which make up the store.

In our little adding operation of $3 + 4 = 7$, which we described just now, we stored 3 in register A, 4 in register B and 7 in register C. Where do you think we stored the instruction which reads:

> "ADD the number in B to the number in A, and put the sum in C"?

(We write this "ADD/A/B/C" for brevity's sake.)

15. We must have another register, D say.
20. In C.
16. In B.

from 15

ADD/A/B/C means "add the number in B to the number in A and place the result in C".

For the computer to do all this for us, we need to be able to tell it *exactly* what we want done. The computer is like an obedient, but literal-minded, servant who does exactly what we tell him, no more and no less.

We tell the computer what to do by *writing down* the *instructions* and the *numbers*. We do, in fact, the *equivalent* of writing out each instruction, very carefully; and then, when our "obedient servant", the computer, is clear about all the instructions, we give him the numbers to work on.

The equivalent of "our written instructions" for the computer is *punched tape* or *punched card*. These are lengths of tape or sets of cards which can be thought of as ruled into squares, and where each square may, or may not, have a hole punched on it. A punched hole and a square with no hole are the symbols from which we make up the language for the computer.

Frames 18 and 19 show pictures of punched tape and a punched card.

Go to **18**

from 7

Correct. $8 - 4 = 4$ and so far your questions have been a little too easy.

To subtract a number from another number is the same as adding it, provided the *sign* of one of the numbers is changed, e.g. $8 + 4 = 12$, and $8 + (-4)$ or $8 - 4 = 4$.

The decision whether to add, subtract, etc., in the computer depends on the *control*. The control in the computer carries out all executive operations (instructions) in the computer.

Suppose we send 12 and -4 to the arithmetic unit with the instruction to ADD, what result shall we expect?

Go to **13**

from 4

No. The addition is $3 + 4 = 7$. The subtraction $8 - 7 = 1$.

Now, we will sometimes ask you to go back to a question and try it again, and sometimes we will not. This time we will, so return to **4**.

from 11

Adding 12 to -4 gives 8, and is the same as subtracting 4 from 12.

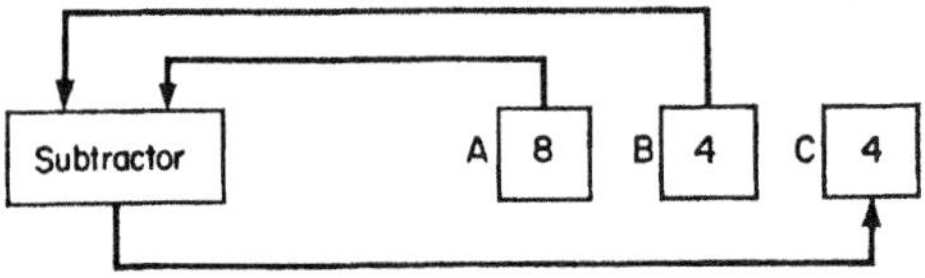

Here is our representation of a subtraction:

Notice one *vital* point about our simple diagram:

> *Each register (the place where the numbers are stored) has an address A, B, C to identify it, and this must* NOT *be confused with the number in the register.*

An address is merely a way of labelling a register to make sure we know how to refer to it, in much the same way as the address of a house enables us to send letters to it.

Which register in our diagram contains 8?

Turn to **6**

from 4

No. $3 + 4 = 7$ and $8 - 7 = 1$ so the correct answer is 1. We shall not normally tell you the correct answer when you are wrong; instead we will ask you to go back and choose between the remaining alternatives, or perhaps go to some entirely new frame.

Anyway, return to **4**, and we hope you will know now which answer to select.

from 9/20

In another register (D say) is the correct answer.

We need another register. We must have registers to store both instructions and numbers. One of our problems in programming our computer lies in deciding in what registers our instructions and numbers should be stored.

But before we start to describe in detail the way in which a digital computer works, let us briefly outline, *by analogy*, the principles on which such large and very fast computers work. They are many thousands of times faster in their operations than human beings and this is the main reason for using them.

Let us look at the whole matter this way. We want our computer to add and subtract numbers for us and to do more complicated mathematics besides, most of which can be reduced to adding and subtracting, and we want it to organize and file information, so that we can keep our account books, and such like, by using a computer rather than a human accountant.

What does ADD/A/B/C mean?

Turn to **10**

16

from 9

No. B already contains a number, and cannot contain an instruction at the same time.

In practice, computers often use separate registers for instructions and numbers so there can be no confusion over this point.

Return to **9**

17

from 7

No.

$$8 + 4 = 12$$
$$8 - 4 = 4$$

You were asked to subtract the contents of B from the contents of A. A contained 8 and B contained 4, so your answer is incorrect.

Return to **7** and try again

18

from 10

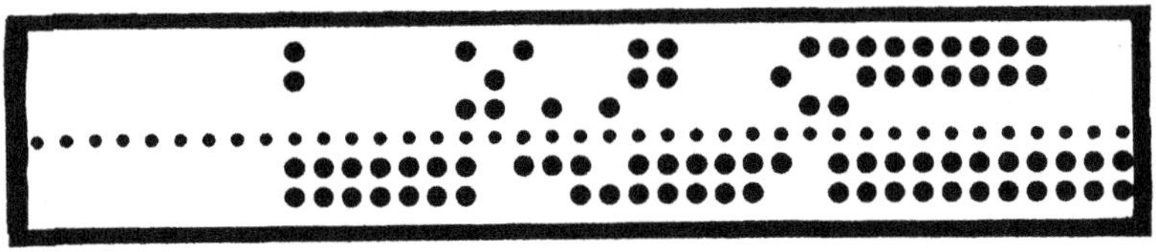

PUNCHED TAPE

Now look at **19**

19

from 18

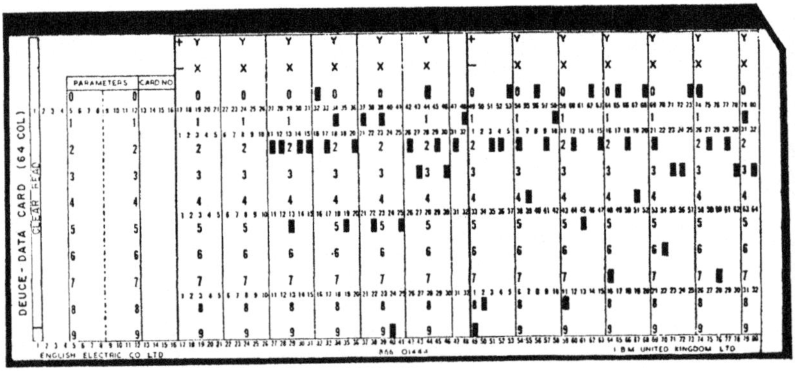

PUNCHED CARD

This card is for *instructions* and we have another one for *numbers*.

Turn to **21**

from 9

No. *C* is already in use, because it contains the number 7. We could not very well use *C* at the same time to contain the instruction that involved the use of itself.

If *A*(3) (let us read this as "*A* contains 3") and *C*(7), then we need a new register *D*, say, so that *D* contains the instruction to add.

Go to **15**

from 19

You must remember that our computer is *automatic*. It is not quite like a desk calculator, where you yourself keep on pressing buttons. We put all the instructions and numbers inside the computer first, and then let it carry on with the job.

What are the means of putting information into the computer?

Turn to **22**

from 21

The information is fed into the computer by punched tape or punched card.

Punched tape is made up of squares, *with* holes punched in them or *without* holes punched in them. A hole stands for *one*, and no-hole stands for *zero*. This is the basis of the simplest code (called Binary Code) into which all numbers and ordinary words can be translated. It is rather like Braille and is read by the computer by *sensing* whether a hole is in a square or not. Binary code is used because it is simple to have switches which only need to represent *two* different states such as 0 and 1, and also because it is so easy to represent two symbols like 0 and 1 on paper.

Try answering the following question:

What is a well-known example of binary code for translating ordinary language?

25. Semaphore—a language which represents symbols by two signal arms which may take up many different positions.
29. Shorthand.
32. Morse code.

from 32

A store is composed of *registers*, each with its own *address*.

One point about computer terminology: we call both our instructions and our numbers *words*. A word is a collection of symbols used by a programmer (the person who decides what instructions and what numbers the computer shall use). Most computers use binary code, so a word for a computer will normally be a set of 0's and 1's like

0110110111

But we shall explain the technical details later. We should also warn you that some computers do not work on computer words in quite this way, although the majority do.

What is the alternative to a punched card as a method of input in the computer?

Look at **24**

from 23

Punched tape can be used as a method of input.

Let us then recapitulate on what we have said so far.

A *store* is the very heart of the computer and it must retain information inside the computer long enough to carry out computations automatically (i.e. without human interference). It has inside it instructions telling it to add, subtract, or whatever operation is needed, and also numbers which are the things added or subtracted.

What is a programmer?

Turn to **28**

25

from 22

No. You may not have known before that semaphore is a visual language, which has two signal arms (rather like those used on the railway) and these can take up many different positions, to represent letters of the alphabet. The fact that it has two arms, both of which may take up *many* positions, ensures that it is not binary.

If it had only *two* positions, as in fact a railway signal has, then it certainly would be in binary code.

Turn to **27**

26

from 29

You could have Morse code with only *dots*. But you *might* agree that the *pause* is also a symbol so you really need two symbols at least, for any language.

This is really a matter of how you wish to use the word "symbol". (You do not count any points for this question whatever your answer.)

Go to **32**

27

from 25

Remember Morse code is a code which uses dots and dashes, and therefore seems like a binary code.

To see what we said to those who answered "Morse code", go to **32**.

28

from 24

A programmer is a person who is responsible for setting out the instructions and numbers in their correct sequence, and then allocating addresses to each instruction and each number.

The address is merely the name given to the particular register where a particular instruction or number is stored.

If we had three numbers 1, 2 and 3 in registers *A*, *B* and *C*, and we wanted simply to add 1 to 2, and then add the result to 3, how many instructions should we expect to use?

30 Two.
34. One.

from 22

Shorthand, you say.

Most shorthand systems use a number of different symbols, certainly more than two, so this is not the answer we had in mind.

Could you communicate a message by using only *one* symbol?

Turn to **26**

from 28/34

Two is correct.

We only need to *add*, but we need to add twice.

So we say ADD 1 to 2 and then ADD (the result of adding 1 to 2) to 3.

Now remember that address *A* contains the number 1, address *B* the number 2 and address *C* the number 3. Let us store the result of the first addition in the store with address *D* and the final result in the store with address *E*. Now that we have allocated all the stores that we need for our numbers, code the two ADD instructions in the form that we have already used.

Turn to **35**

from 40

An address is the name of the location, in store, of a number or an instruction.

Look at this very simple block diagram of a digital computer:

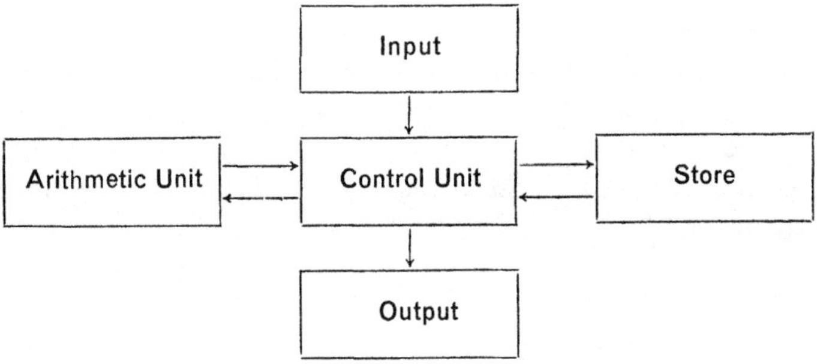

This is almost the simplest possible representation of a complete digital computer.

We could put a great deal more detail into our diagram, but we could not make it much simpler and yet still more or less *complete*.

Go to **36**

from 22/26/27

Morse code is the correct answer.

Morse code provides a binary code, into which any language can be translated. You might argue that Morse code normally uses three symbols—dot, dash and pause. This makes it a ternary rather than a binary code, but we accept morse code as the correct answer.

A computer takes in instructions and numbers, usually in binary code, and stores both the instructions and the numbers. For this, the computer must have a storage system that retains the information.

It is often convenient to think of an ordinary file as a storage system. But we have said that a store is composed of . . ., each with its own . . .

Fill in the missing words and then turn to **23**.

from 35

E contains $3 + 3 = 6$.

Although a digital computer is electronic and automatic, and it represents 1's and 0's by electronic pulses, and usually uses electronic or magnetic stores, it can be thought of in many different ways.

As one analogy, we recommend that the reader thinks of a filing cabinet with a desk calculator inside one of the files.

When the reader is thinking of the *automatic* operation of the computer he should have in mind something like a railway system which is automatically controlled by signals.

A desk calculator is manual and not automatic. Is this statement true or false?

37. False.
40. True.

from 28

The one instruction would have to tell you to add twice. In general, although we only need the single instruction word *to add*, we have to use it twice.

So we have to say

ADD 1 to 2 and ADD $(1 + 2)$ to 3

meaning this to be carried out by two instructions.

Go to **30**

35

from 30

ADD/A/B/D
ADD/D/C/E
What number have we now got in E?

Go to **33**

from 31

General view of a digital computer.

This is the I.C.T. 1301 computer with card reader, card punch, paper tape reader and paper tape punch. The magnetic tape store is on the right of the picture. The cabinets at the back contain the *power pack*; the girl is seated at the *control panel.*

The *power pack* contains the source of electrical power which is necessary to allow the computer to operate.

The *control panel* is the point where the programmer can control the computer's input and output and interfere with its operations should she want to.

Now go to **38**

from 33

No, it is quite true.

A desk calculator is not automatic because it has no store. At least it can store, in a sense, only the numbers it has immediately in its arithmetic unit. Certainly without an information store, no system whatever could be automatic.

Go to **40**

from 36

This is the end of our first chapter which has simply outlined the simplest relationship between the input and the store and the arithmetic unit. The control carries out the instructions and transfers numbers from store into the arithmetic unit, to be operated upon, and then transfers the results back into store.

The computer operates automatically, and represents both numbers and instructions (these are both called computer *words*) in binary code, a language of 0's and 1's.

The computer also has an input and an output, and for this purpose usually uses punched cards or punched tape. This has to be read by a sensing device in the computer, much as a blind man reads braille.

Now to learn more about these points go to **41** and begin Chapter Two.

from 41

Remember, we can think of storing our computer *words* (of two kinds) in our file, and this is our storage. It could be a box full of cards, but because it is electronic, it happens to be in the form of *electrical pulses*, and magnetized spots on *magnetic drums*, *magnetic tape* or *magnetic discs*. But you can think of it, for all practical purposes, as a set of cards in a file.

One vital point about this: we store these cards, but the computer needs to *refer* to them, as it goes through its instructions, and therefore *each card must have an address*. The addresses will ultimately be in binary code.

How many different digits are there in binary code?

Think of the answer, then turn to **42**

from 33/37

False is the correct answer.

A desk calculator is manual. It is, in effect, an arithmetic unit which could be said to store the numbers as you calculate with them, but a computer stores numbers *and* instructions.

No system could be automatic without a store. The fact of having a store is no guarantee that it will be automatic, but if the system contains both instructions and data (numbers), then it may operate over a period of time without human interference and it is this property we call "automatic".

What is an address?

Turn to **31**

from 38

CHAPTER TWO

Programming and the Control Unit

THIS chapter follows up in depth the general survey of Chapter One, and places special emphasis on *programming* and on the workings of the computer *control unit*.

Turn to 39

from 39

Binary code has two different *digits* and they are 0 and 1.

The easiest method of addressing (still using decimal code for the moment) would be to label our pack of cards consecutively, starting at 0. Then the instruction on card 1 might tell the computer to add the number on card 11 to the number on card 10, and put the result on card 12. If we use a code for ADD (01, say), then we can write this instruction as

1. 01/10/11/12

(Note that the 1. at the beginning means "The instruction written on card 1 is . . .".)

What then shall we expect to find printed on card 1?

45. 01/10/11/12.
49. 1. 01/10/11/12.
51. 1. 01.

from 45

No.

$$8 + 12 = 20$$
$$20 + 40 = 60$$
$$60 - 15 = 45$$
$$45 \div 5 = 9$$

You probably made your mistake on the last step and said $45 - 5 = 40$.

Turn to **47**

from 47

$$\frac{[(8 + 12) + 40] - 15}{5}$$

It is easy to see the correct sequence of operation:

(1) $8 + 12 = 20$
(2) $20 + 40 = 60$
(3) $60 - 15 = 45$
(4) $45 \div 5 = 9$

Then the computer can be made to *print out* the answer 9, but leave that for now.

Write down next the computer instructions of our problem (not in coded form, but ordinary language).

Then turn to **46**

from 42/49

The correct answer is 01/10/11/12. We think card 1 may be so numbered in the corner, but what is *certainly* printed on it will be 01/10/11/12.

The next point to be made is on *programming*, and the construction of this instruction 01/10/11/12 is precisely a part of programming. Programming is an essential part of any course on computers, and we will remind you again that *programming* is the arranging and organizing of all the instructions that make up the programme in a computer.

Look at this problem:

> Add 12 to 8, then add the sum to 40. Take away 15 and divide the result by 5.

It is an easy problem which you could do in your head, but we will show you how to programme a computer to do it for you.

What is the final arithmetic answer?

43. 40.
47. 9.

from 44

Now the instructions are:

1. ADD contents of *B* to contents of *A* and place the answer in *A*. (*The placing of the sum of A and B in A "wipes out" the original number in A.*)
2. Now ADD contents of *C* to contents of *A*, and place answer in *A* again.
3. Now SUBTRACT contents of *D* from contents of *A*, and place answer in *A*.
4. Now DIVIDE contents of *A* by contents of *E*, and place the answer in *A*.
5. PRINT out the contents of *A*. (We also need an instruction for STOP, but we shall not include this at the moment.)

Proceed to **48**

from 43/45

9 is the correct answer.

Now imagine the following simple computer having storage registers with addresses *A*, *B*, *C*, *D* and *E* for *numbers*. The numbers can be placed in, and taken out of, the arithmetic unit. The other registers contain the instructions which control the operations performed on the numbers.

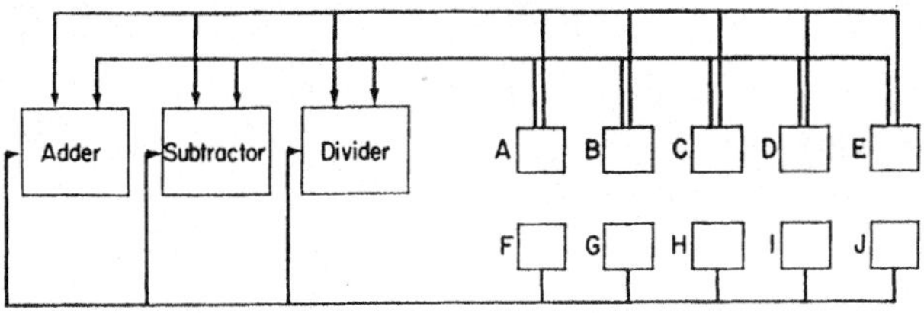

Now we have our numbers in the registers, 8 in *A*, 12 in *B*, 40 in *C*, 15 in *D* and 5 in *E*. (Make a note of this.) We have the instructions in the other registers.

Write down the computation in mathematical form. You can store a number in a register which already has a number in it, but you will then delete the old number.

Turn to **44**

from 46

Let us show you a *flow diagram*, as we call it, for this simple programme.

We use circles for starts and stops, and squares or rectangles for the other steps.

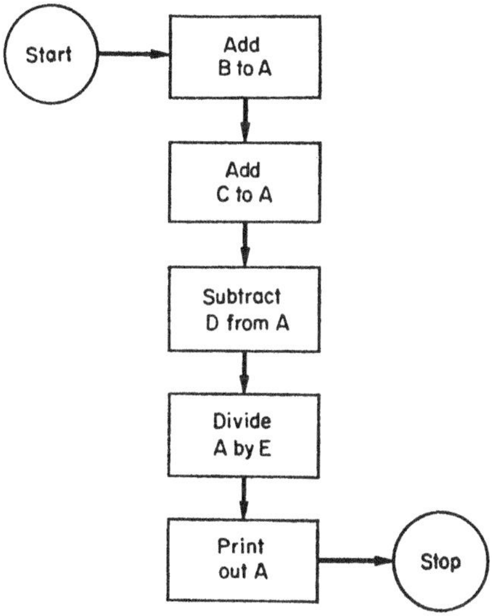

A (8)
B (12)
C (40)
D (15)
E (5)

and place result of each operation in *A*.

What does the circle mean in a flow diagram?

Turn to **50**

from 42

You turn to card 1 and see

1. 01/10/11/12

and you read this as "This is card 1, and you add (01) the number on card 11 to the number on card 10 and write the result on card 12".

This is fair enough. We think, though, that you would not start with 1. at the beginning and would rather keep the number on the card itself separate from the instruction. However, count full marks if this was your first choice, and

Go to **45**

from 48

A circle in a flow diagram represents a start or a stop.

We shall not write the phrase "the contents of", but simply say

ADD B to A and put the result in C
ADD/A/B/C,

or ADD A to B and put the result in C
ADD/B/A/C.

(We should notice ADD/A/B/C means "add B to A and place result in C".)

(We really mean, of course, here by A, the *contents of A*.)

If SUB is short for subtract, what is the instruction for subtracting B from A and putting the result in C?

Write down the answer and turn to **52**

from 42

If you turn to card 1, you are acting as a control in effect, and you are looking for instructions to be obeyed. You read 1. 01 and you could read this as "This is card 1, ADD". But *what* do you add?

This is obviously not enough information.

Return to **42** and try again

from 50

SUB/*A*/*B*/*C* means "subtract *B* from *A* and place result in *C*".

Similarly, DIV/*A*/*B*/*C* means "divide *A* by *B* and place result in *C*". So the programme is, by inference,

ADD/*A*/*B*/*A*
ADD/*A*/*C*/*A*
SUB/*A*/*D*/*A*
DIV/*A*/*E*/*A*

What does DIV/*A*/*B*/*C* mean?

Go to **56**

from 61

Seven registers, you say.

Now we have

200(4)
201(5)
202(2)
203(20)
204 (the result of adding 4 to 5)
205 (the result of multiplying contents of 204 by 2)
206 (the result of subtracting contents of 205 from 20).

That is *seven* instructions for numbers only.

Now we need *three* more for add, multiply and subtract *and* we need one for print (07). So we need more than seven registers. You must be clear that numbers and instructions *both* have their own addresses.

As a separate problem, let us assume that we had two instructions dealing with *eight* numbers.

How many registers in our store should we fill?

58. Two.
65. Eight.
69. Ten.

from 56

03/*A*/*B*/*C* means "multiply the number in *A* by the number in *B* and put the result in *C*".

Let us remember that the programmer must perform the following operations:

(1) He must be clear what the programme is intended to achieve.
(2) He must be able to deal with all the arithmetical problems that arise.
(3) He must draw up a *flow diagram*.
(4) He must translate the instructions into computer form (e.g. 01/*A*/*B*/*C*).
(5) He must code the programme.
(6) Then he must test it.

Would you normally expect a programme to work first time on the computer?

Turn to **57**

from 57

A programmer has to *organize* the total programme. He has to arrange the instructions properly, code them and test the programme. This is vital because the computer must work automatically.

A digital computer is automatic by virtue of being able to *store* a great deal of information involving both instructions and numbers. If it had no store, it could not be automatic.

Is this last statement true or false?

59. False.
62. True.

from 52

DIV/A/B/C means "divide the number in address A by the number in B and put the result in C".

If we now use the codes

01 for ADD
02 for SUB
04 for DIV

(03 would now be saved for *multiply*, or MUL), we can now present the coded programme in the form

01/A/B/A
01/A/C/A
02/A/D/A
04/A/E/A

and further instructions for PRINT and STOP.

What does 03/A/B/C mean?

Turn to **54**

from 54

No.

A *new* programme requires "debugging". It has to be tested step by step by controlling the computer by way of switches at the control panel or console. Each instruction is put through separately and the stores are checked to see that they have changed appropriately.

Programming is a specialized and skilled job.

What would you say, in general terms, a programmer had to do?

Turn to 55

from 53

Two registers will be needed merely for the instructions and eight for the numbers, so two will *not* be enough, since *both* instructions *and* numbers need registers with their own addresses.

Return to **53**

---

from 55

No. It is true.

The point is that a computer can store *both* numbers and instructions, and this is what distinguishes it as being automatic.

Turn to **62**

from 61

Twelve, you say.

Well, we have 200 to 206 for numbers (that is seven registers). We need a print instruction (07) and that is one single instruction. We also need three instructions for add, multiply and subtract. This does *not* add up to 12.

Return to **61**

from 63/69

Three, for purely mathematical purposes.

You will also need input instructions, to place the numbers *and* instructions in store, and you will also need a print instruction (07) to print out the result.

We will not bother with the input instructions, but we will assume our results at each stage go in 204, 205 and 206 and we print out the contents of 206. (We have 200(4), 201(5), 202(2) and 203(20) already, where 200(4) means that "register with address 200 contains the number 4".)

How many registers shall we need for the whole operation (excluding input and stop instructions)?

53. Seven.
60. Twelve.
64. Eleven.

from 55/59

The correct answer is "true". If a computer is automatic, then it must have a store.

A desk calculator may be said to store numbers, but it normally only does so for a very short time. A computer stores *both* numbers and instructions, for *any* length of time.

Now, do we have to place both the instructions and the numbers in store before the computer operates?

Turn to **63**

from 62

Well, it may not be necessary, since the instructions may operate upon the numbers as they arrive in store. However, think of both as being stored.

This is a most important point. Suppose you have a simple programme such as

> "Add 4 to 5, multiply the result by 2 and subtract the next result from 20."

Although this is a simple problem, it nevertheless requires careful planning.

If you place 4 in register with address 200, 5 in register 201, 2 in 202, and 20 in 203, how many instructions will you need?

Turn to **61**

64

from 61

Quite right.

We place our numbers in registers. There are *seven* registers for these (200–206). We have *three* registers for the mathematical instructions, and we have *one* register for the print instruction (07).

Never forget that once we have placed all the numbers in addresses, we must construct the instructions to refer to them and *then* place the instructions in further addresses.

Turn to **66**

65

from 53

Eight registers are needed for the *numbers* alone, according to our plan, and we also need two for the *instructions*, so eight is not enough.

Return to **53**

from 64

What is the programme we need in order to

> "Add 4 to 5, multiply the result by 2, and subtract the next result from 20"?

Given 200(4), 201(5), 202(2), 203(20) and the first result in 204, the second in 205 and the third and final result in 206.

Our instructions can go in 000, 001 and 002. What are these instructions?

68. 000. 01/005/004/009
001. 03/009/002/018
002. 02/020/018/002

70. 000. 01/200/201/204
001. 03/204/202/205
002. 02/205/203/206

75. 000. 01/201/200/204
001. 03/204/202/205
002. 02/203/205/206

from 78

This answer contains a simple error.
Look again:

PRINT/*A*/*B*/*C* or 07/*A*/*B*/*C* where *A*(7) and $B = 202$ means "print the 7 words starting at register with address 202, and take the next instruction from address *C*".

Return to **78**

from 66

Your answer would be quite correct *if* instructions referred to numbers, rather than the addresses of the numbers.

But instructions refer to the address of a register and *not* its contents.

Return to **66** and try the question again

from 53

Two instructions and eight numbers require ten registers. So you are correct.

Never forget that once we have placed all the numbers in addresses, we must construct the instructions to refer to them and *then* place the instructions in further addresses.

Return to **61** and answer the original question

70

from 66

There are two mistakes here.

The basic mistake in each case is that in an arithmetical (or mathematical) instruction such as ADD/*A*/*B*/*C* it is always *B* that is "active" and added (subtracted, etc.) to *A*, and not vice-versa.

Return to **66**

71

from 78

You must *never* confuse the address of a register with its contents, even though we *could* have used such a PRINT instruction.

If 200(4), which means "register with address 200 contains the number 4", then any instruction which uses this 4 (in 200) will refer to 200 and *not* to 4.

Return to **78**

from 77

Correct.

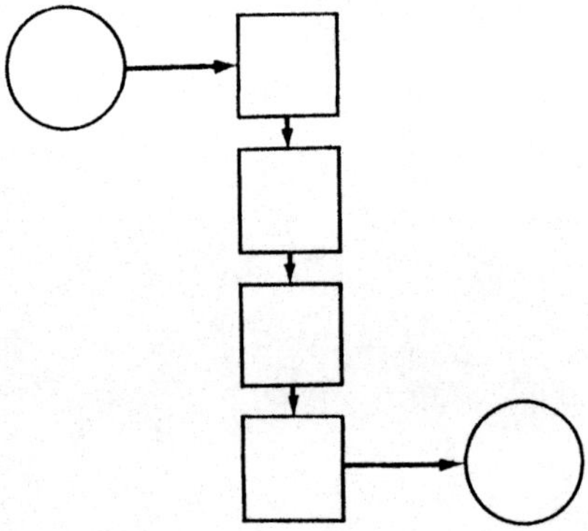

Now draw the flow diagram on a piece of paper and then fill in the circles and squares with a brief description of our last programme, where we added 4 to 5, multiplied the result by 2, subtracted the result of the multiplication from 20 and printed out the result.

When you have done this, turn to **80**

from 77

A *simple* flow diagram looks like the following:

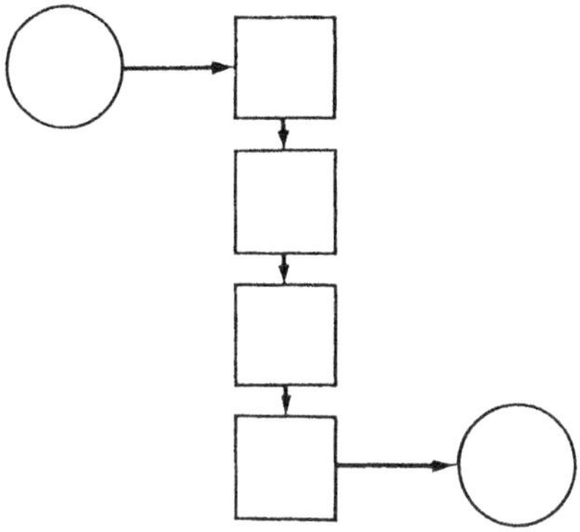

So you are wrong.

Return to **77** and try again

---

from 78

Well done. 07/205/204/000 (where 205 contains 5) means "print 5 consecutive words starting with address 204, and take the next instruction in address 000".

Now consider the very first steps of our computer programming operation. Assuming we have no mathematical problems and we are clear what it is we have to achieve, what is our next step?

Write down the answer and turn to **77**

from 66

Quite right. 000. 01/201/200/204 means

> "In register 000, we have an instruction to add the contents of 200 to the contents of 201 and place the result in 204."

This is $5 + 4 = 9$.

Then 001. 03/204/202/205 multiplies 9 by 2 where 204(9) and 202(2); the result (18) goes in 205.

Then $20 - 18 = 2$. This is the final result which is placed in register 206, and which is printed out.

PRINT/*A*/*B*/*C* means "print *n* consecutive words (where *n* is the number in register *A*) starting from the register with the address *B*, and take the next instruction from address *C*". (Remember that each register contains one word.)

Now, applying this to the above calculation, if we say that *A* contains the number 1, and *B* is register 206, what will the computer actually print out?

Go on to **76**

from 75

The computer will print one word starting at address 206, i.e. it will print out the content of 206.

This sort of instruction such as PRINT is an organizational instruction and uses addresses rather differently from an arithmetical instruction.

So to be sure you understand this sort of instruction, look again at PRINT/*A*/*B*/*C*. It means:

> "Take the *number in A* (or you can use *A* itself here as the number) and print that number of words starting at register with address *B* and printing the words consecutively, then take the next instruction in address *C*."

For example, if 208(5), then the instruction PRINT/208/203/000 means "print the 5 words from registers 203, 204, 205, 206 and 207, then take the instruction in 000".

If 209(3), what does 07/209/280/000 mean?

Turn to **78**

from 74

You will draw a *flow diagram* next. You will have *starts* and *stops* and many arithmetical steps in between.

What symbols do we use for (i) starts, (ii) stops, (iii) in-between steps?

72. (i) Circles, (ii) circles, (iii) squares.
73. (i) Circles, (ii) squares, (iii) squares.
90. (i) Squares, (ii) circles, (iii) squares.

from 76

If 209(3), 07/209/280/000 means "print 3 consecutive words starting from register 280 (i.e. 280, 281, 282), then take the instruction in 000".

In other words PRINT/*A*/*B*/*C* means PRINT *a* consecutive words (where *a* is the number in address *A*) starting at *B*, then go to *C*. *The code for* PRINT *is* 07.

If we wanted to print *five* consecutive words starting at register 204, and then to take the next instruction from 000, what would the instruction be, assuming the number 5 is in 205?

67. 07/204/205/000.
71. 07/005/204/000.
74. 07/205/204/000.

from 85/87

Yes, it certainly can subtract numbers even if it does not have a subtractor.

Subtraction is addition, where at least one of the numbers is negative. So we say $a-b$ is the same as $a + (-b)$.

So subtraction is perfectly possible provided we can represent *negative* numbers in our computer: this we do by using what we call a *sign digit*.

But before we discuss *sign digits*, we must tell you that all *computer words* (representing numbers and instructions) are made up of digits. The numerals one, two, three, etc., are represented by the digits 1, 2, 3, and we have ten different digits (symbols) in our ordinary system. We have already used the term "digit" in talking of two digits (0 and 1) being used in binary code, but we shall now test you a little on the word "digit".

Which are the ten *different* digits (symbols) we normally use?

86. 1, 10, 20, 30, 40, 50, 60, 70, 80, 90.
89. 0, 1, 2, 3, 4, 5, 6, 7, 8, 9.
93. 1, 2, 3, 4, 5, 6, 7, 8, 9, 10.

from 72

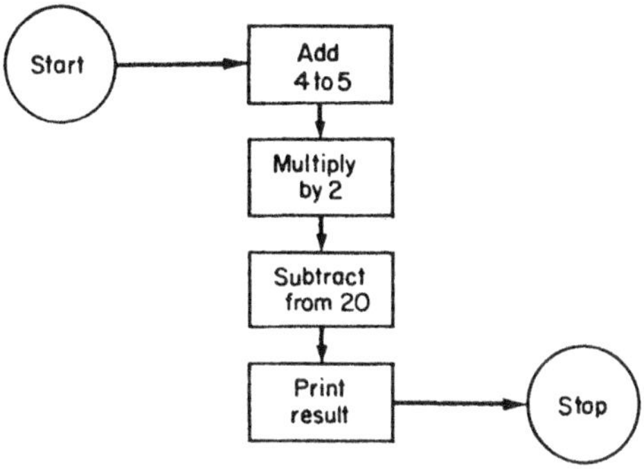

You can now allocate registers to numbers and code the instructions, then allocate stores to instructions.

Turn to **81**

from 80

We have been using a computer (one which we have made up for the purpose) with 3-*address* instructions.

The 3-address instruction word is of the form $F/A/B/C$, where F is the function and A, B and C are the three addresses.

What sort of computer (1-address, 2-address or 3-address) might we expect to use with this type of instruction?

Turn to **82**

from 81

A 3-address instruction is certainly intended for a 3-address computer.

A 1-address computer needs to refer only to one *register* which is where all numbers are sent for the purpose of doing Arithmetic. Such a special register is called an *accumulator*. A register, we will remind you, is the name for the place in storage where *words* are kept—they can be thought of as cards, if you do not want to think in terms of electronics.

Now a 3-address computer names three addresses: two numbers for the two addresses where numbers are to be taken from (to be added together for example) and one for the address where the sum is to be put.

A 2-address computer is something of a compromise, but, as in the case of a 1-address computer, an *accumulator* is normally used.

What is the *form* of the instruction to ADD in a 3-address computer?

Go to **84**

from 84

A 2-address computer instruction is of the form $F/A/B$.
Here is another computer, the I.C.T. 1300 digital computer.

Turn to **85**

from 82

ADD/*A*/*B*/*C*.

We should summarize some more of our knowledge of computers.

Digital computers can be of at least three different types. They can be

1-address,
2-address,
or 3-address.

They usually use *binary code*, although they may sometimes use numerical codes based on other numbers of digits (e.g. the octal code, which uses the eight digits, 0–7).

Instructions and *numbers* have to be *coded*, and the programmer organizes the information for the computer first by using a *flow diagram* to represent his problem.

What is the form of a 2-address computer instruction?

Turn to **83**

from 83

A digital computer performs a whole set of *mathematical operations*, such as addition, multiplication, finding square roots, and so on. This means that it must have a *store* in which to place the sets of *numbers* to be operated on, as well as the instructions which state what the nature of the operation is—whether addition, division or whatever.

It performs all these operations automatically, so we have to put in all the information first (instructions and numbers) and then let it run until it prints out the answers, provided, of course, we remember to include the *instruction* to print out the answers. Whatever we wish the computer to do, we must always instruct it, *precisely*, to do it.

Now it must have means of storing *words*, this being the name we use for both the instructions and the numbers.

Can a digital computer *subtract* numbers even if it has no subtractor?

79. Yes.
87. No.

from 79

You say 1, 10, 20, 30, 40, 50, 60, 70, 80, 90.

No. This is not correct. This set of numbers includes combinations of digits such as 10, 20, etc.

This collection of numbers certainly *includes* the ten digits we normally use; they are

0, 1, 2, 3, 4, 5, 6, 7, 8, and 9.

But this was not the question.

Return to **79** and look at the question again; then try another answer.

from 85

No. You are wrong. It *can* subtract.

But to do so it needs to be able to represent negative numbers, and then it becomes the same as addition:

$$a - b = a + (-b)$$

A negative number is usually represented by a *sign digit*.

Go to **79**

from 94

Words in a computer are collections of symbols or digits. There are two kinds of words. One kind is made up of digits representing numbers, the other kind uses the *same* digits as symbols, in a code representing instructions.

Thus 1 2 4 6 5 9 2 4 is an eight-digit word which may represent a number, and a pretty big number too! It may, however, represent an instruction which tells the computer what to do. Let us suppose that 12 means "find common factors" and that 465 and 924 are the *addresses* of the numbers whose common factors are to be found. *Notice that an address such as* 465 *tells us where, in the computer, a particular number may be found*, but it does *not* tell us what the number is—it may be anything.

What does 12/240/241/242 mean?

Write down the answer and turn to **96**

89

from 79

0, 1, 2, 3, 4, 5, 6, 7, 8, 9 is correct. This is called the *decimal system* of numbers.

But although there are ten different digits involved, you should notice that the digits in a number can be repeated any number of times.

The following number, for example, has seven digits:

1 1 0 2 3 4 1

How many digits has this number?

1 1 1 1 1 1 1 1 1 1

91. One.
94. Ten.

90

from 77

A *simple* flow diagram looks like the following:

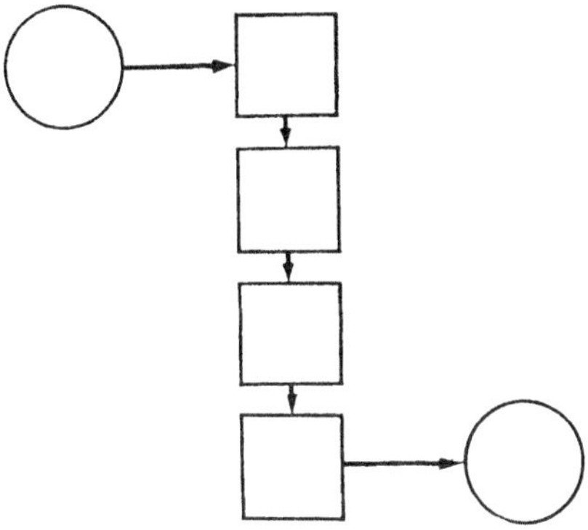

So you are wrong.

Return to **77** and try again.

91

from 89

One is wrong. It uses one symbol, the digit 1.
The answer should have been ten.

Go to **94**

92

from 96

According to our own agreed convention,

1 2 4 6 5 9 2 4 stands for −2 4 6 5 9 2 4

so now you can see the correct answer easily enough, which is not the one you chose.

It is, of course, that + 2 4 6 5 9 2 4 is represented by 0 2 4 6 5 9 2 4.

Go to **95**

93

from 79

You say 1, 2, 3, 4, 5, 6, 7, 8, 9, 10.

But the word "digit" means here the single symbols used, and 10 is a *combination* of symbols made up of the two digits 1 and 0.

So you are wrong in choosing this set of ten numbers.

Return to **79**, and reconsider the question.

from 89/91

Ten is correct.

The digit (or symbol) 1 is repeated ten times, so we say that 1 1 1 1 1 1 1 1 1 1 has ten digits. In the same way the numbers 246, 35 and 2426 have three, two and four digits respectively.

On the other hand 246 uses three *different* digits (symbols), but 2426 also only uses three *different* digits.

Go to **88**

from 92/96

0 2 4 6 5 9 2 4 is correct since 0 says the number is *positive*.

So quite clearly the first digit of *our number word is never* a *digit of the number the word represents.* It always tells you whether the number, which is represented by the word, is + or − (positive or negative).

What is 1 2 3 4 5 6 7 8 as a number?

Turn to **97**

from 88

12/240/241/242 means "Find common factors of numbers in 240 and 241, and put common factors into 242."

We were going to tell you about a sign digit, and we shall now do so. This is usually the *first digit* of the *number word*, which indicates whether the number is positive or negative, so if we use 1 2 4 6 5 9 2 4 to represent a number, let us suppose that 1 stands for a negative number, and 0 for a positive number. (We can use more complicated conventions for the sign digit, which may state whether or not letters appear among the numbers and other conventionally imparted information, but we shall keep solely to a designation of the sign of the number.)

How, in the light of our convention, could we represent + 2 4 6 5 9 2 4?

92. 1 2 4 6 5 9 2 4.
95. 0 2 4 6 5 9 2 4.

from 95

1 2 3 4 5 6 7 8 is −2 3 4 5 6 7 8 in our sign convention.

Now let us summarize what we have said so far.

A digital computer stores information in its *store*, then it automatically operates on the numbers by adding them, subtracting them, and so on and so forth.

The computer has its own language which is called *binary code*, having only two different symbols 0 and 1.

Words are collections of digits, of which there are two kinds, instruction words and number words, or, as we sometimes call them, *instruction words* and *data words*.

The *programmer* organizes the data by preparing flow diagrams, and allocating registers to numbers, and then the instructions that refer to the numbers.

The part of the computer that controls the carrying out of the programme is called the —— ——.

Fill in the blanks and turn to **98**

from 97

Control Unit

The control unit is composed of the instruction register and sequence control register, at the very least.

Naturally, since scientific and business experts use computers, a great deal of specialists' jargon has grown up around the computer, and much of our time will be spent explaining this terminology. Much of it, though, is sensibly chosen. Such as *words*, *address*, *binary*, *code*, *store*, *input*, *output*, *punched card* and *punched tape*. But there is a lot more to come, and as with any new subject, a good deal of effort is spent on learning a new specialized language.

Binary-to-decimal converter, too, is fairly self-explanatory. It converts binary numbers like 10000 into decimal numbers like 16.

The whole computer programme is run by the *control unit*, and the computer instruction being operated at any moment is in what?

100. Sequence control register.
103. Instruction register.

99

from 103

The sequence control register (S.C.R.) contains the *address* of the instruction “add the number in 200 to the number in 201 and put the result in 202”, and we have *not* yet said *where* the instruction is placed.

If it is in register 008, then the S.C.R. contains the number 008.

What does the instruction register (I.R.) contain?

Go to **101**

100

from 98

The sequence control register contains the *address* of the instruction which is being operated upon; this instruction is in the instruction register.

Turn to **103** to see the frame which you would have seen had you been right first time.

101

from 99

The I.R. contains the details of the instruction, which we can code as

01/201/200/202

i.e. "add the number in 200 to the number in 201 and put the result in 202."

The control unit is composed of the instruction register and sequence control register.

Is this true or false?

104. True.
107. False.

from 104/106

The S.C.R. adds 1 to the address and transforms the address 246 into 247.

In the meantime the instruction, which is in address 246, is executed by the C.U., and when this is finished, the C.U. will automatically call up the instruction in 247, increase the S.C.R. by 1, in preparation for the instruction in 248, and then carry out the instruction in 247.

Now the I.R. contains the instruction, but what does the S.C.R. contain?

Go to **105**

103

from 98/100

The instruction register contains the instruction being operated upon, and the sequence control register contains its address.

So if the instruction is "add the number in 200 to the number in 201 and put the result in 202", what is in the sequence control register?

Turn to **99**

104

from 101/107

It is true that the control unit (C.U.) is composed of the instruction register (I.R.) and the sequence control register (S.C.R.).

Notice that the S.C.R. "ticks up one" as each instruction is about to be obeyed, so that if the current instruction being operated upon has address 246, what will be the address of the next instruction to be brought into the I.R.?

102. 247.
106. 245.

from 102

The S.C.R. contains the *address* of the instruction which is to be next in the I.R.

Inside our computer, as well as having a storage, you will remember that we also have an arithmetic unit which provides the usual means for adding, subtracting and such like arithmetical operations.

We must now remind you of the analogy which you should bear in mind. Inside the computer we have a control unit, which is like a signal box in a railway system. It organizes the controls, the flow of (trains) information, and where the trains stop is the railway station. In computer language, the railway station is the address of the word, which may contain either instructions or numbers.

Are all the instructions arithmetical?

Turn to **108**

106

from 104

The S.C.R. adds 1 to the address and transforms 246 into 247. So you are not correct.

To see what was said to those who were correct, go to **102**

107

from 101

The control unit (C.U.) *is* composed of the instruction register (I.R.) and the sequence control register (S.C.R.).

So our statement was true and you were wrong.

Go to **104**

from 105

No. There are organizational and input–output instructions as well as arithmetical instructions.

We have said that computer words are represented by combinations of holes punched on tape or card, for the purpose of input and output.

Inside the computer, these punched holes are translated into electrical pulses, which travel from input to the store, and from the store to the arithmetic unit, back to the store to the output, and a copy to the store, and so on and so forth. It is all very much like a network of railway lines, where the word-pulses are the trains.

The C.U. has the job of sending these trains to the right place at the right time. Indeed, the process does seem fairly complicated—but only at first sight.

What does the I.R. contain?

Turn to **109**

from 108

The I.R. contains the instruction currently being obeyed.
Now for a little revision.
A digital computer is made up primarily as follows.

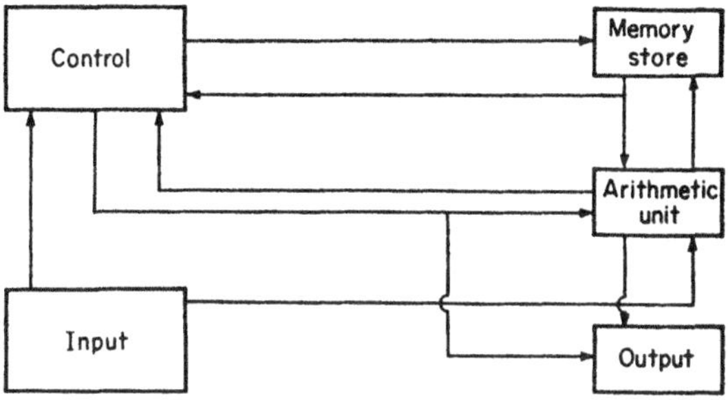

What are the important features of a computer store?

Turn to **113**

from 115

You say, No.

It really is quite true that the computer operates on instructions exactly as it is told to; but you may perhaps be thinking that it sometimes makes mistakes. You may even be thinking that computers are not always given wholly definite instructions. Although this is not the correct answer you are not expected to know this yet, so we are awarding full marks to those who said it was *true*. A computer does precisely what its instructions tell it to do.

Go back to **115** and when you have convinced yourself of the right answer, choose the correct frame in order to continue.

from 113

No. The earliest computers were purely mechanical.

Now computers are of two kinds, *digital* and *analogue*. Digital computers operate in discrete steps (e.g. a typewriter or a desk calculator), whereas analogue computers operate in continuous steps (e.g. a slide rule). We are concerned in this programme with *digital* computers.

A digital computer is like a violin rather than like a piano, in so far as it is discrete in its operations.

Is the above statement true or false?

114. True.
118. False.

from 117

Yes. It can have a store without being automatic, but it cannot be automatic without having a store.

The usual method of dealing with numbers and instructions is to bring them into the temporary high-speed storage just prior to their use. Sometimes the whole programme (which is the total set of instructions) is small enough to be put into the temporary storage alone, but this may not be possible with larger programmes.

Does the use of the slower, larger *auxiliary store* imply the use of a large computer programme?

116. Yes.
119. No.

from 109

The most important features of a computer store are

(1) that it should be fast and efficient;
(2) that it should be capable of storing binary digits which make up *words*;
(3) that the *registers* used for the words should all have addresses.

We have been describing a 3-address automatic electronic *digital* computer.

Does a computer need to be electronic?

Go to **111**

from 111

True, you say. It most certainly is not true.

You must agree that a piano is like a typewriter in so far as it is "*all-or-nothing*," as are all *digital* systems (either a particular note is struck or it is not). A violin can be adjusted with as much precision as you like, and can have notes played which differ minutely from each other in pitch, at the player's will, and it is, therefore, *analogue*.

But we shall not need to worry about this as we are only concerned with *digital* systems from now on.

Go to **118**

from 118

Now the problem of *programming* a computer lies, as we have already said, in working out, *in advance*, exactly what instructions you wish the computer to follow, and what numbers it must process. This makes the computer more like a *pianola* than a piano.

Does an automatic digital computer operate on its instructions exactly as it is told to, and then produce the answer?

110. No.
117. Yes.
120. Do not know.

from 112/119

The correct answer is that the use of the slower, larger *auxiliary store* does imply the use of a large computer programme.

Fairly large anyway, although we all agree that "large" is a very relative term.

Now we have been outlining programming and the operation of the control unit. We need next to discuss the codes used to represent instructions, numbers and addresses in the computer. This is usually binary code, but can you remember any other codes we have mentioned?

Turn to **121**

from 115

Yes. You are correct, although there may be slight variations possible on this general procedure.

But now we must explain a little more about a computer. Look again at the following diagram, which is slightly more complicated than the first block diagram we drew in Chapter One.

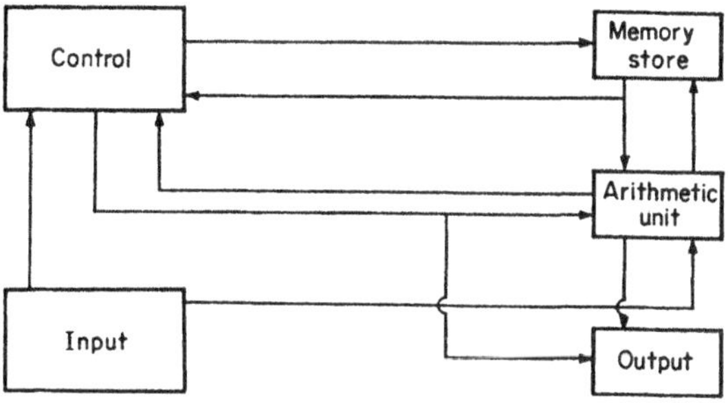

Here we have a *computer storage* system (sometimes called "temporary" store) which operates at *high-speed*, and is too expensive for the complete storage. We also have a larger *auxiliary store* which is *slower* but cheaper, sometimes called a "permanent" store. Modern computers often have a single-stage store, but we shall also describe the two-stage store.

Is a store necessary for a machine to be automatic?

Turn to **112**

from 111/114

False is the correct answer.

A piano is like a typewriter, and is an "all-or-nothing" system, where you either press a key representing a note or you do not press it.

A violin is an analogue system whereby you can make almost any degree of adjustment along a continuous scale of notes. We are dealing only with *digital* systems (one type of "all-or-nothing" system) from now on, and we are also dealing with automatic and electronic systems.

As we have already said, these work automatically in the sense of putting into the machine, right at the beginning, the full set of instructions, telling the machine what mathematical operations to perform. Then the numbers are put in and the machine processes the numbers.

Turn to **115**

119

from 112

Your answer was No. You are wrong.

The use of the *auxiliary store* usually does imply a larger programme, if you accept the purely relative use of the word "larger". Normally, with a short programme you may get all the instructions and numbers in the *temporary* store, and you would not need to bother with the larger *permanent* store.

Go to **116**

120

from 115

You say you do not know. Well the answer is that it does do exactly as it is told.

Sometimes a computer instruction may operate in a contingent manner, so that the carrying out of a particular instruction may be contingent on some particular occurrence. So, to take a simple example, we might instruct the computer to transfer a number from one register to another if, and only if, that number is bigger than some other number. It is as if we said, *when* we get to 20, stop. We shall meet such cases.

Return to **115**

from 116

We have also mentioned *decimal* and *octal* codes (eight-digit codes). There are also *duodecimal* (twelve-digit) and *hexa-decimal* (sixteen-digit) codes, and others which we will not bother you with.

In our next chapter we shall be discussing these codes in greater detail.

Turn to **122**

from 121

CHAPTER THREE

Computer Arithmetic

THIS chapter is concerned with Computer Arithmetic. This means the various arithmetical codes such as binary, octal, decimal, duodecimal and hexadecimal codes.

Now let us ask a question to remind you of the role of the arithmetic unit.

What does it do?

Turn to **124**

from 124

5 is the same in both. They do not differ until they get to 10.

A computer generally uses binary code because it means that only two symbols 0 and 1 have to be represented inside the computer, and this can be done by simple two-stage switches. Although this makes the numbers rather longer, the *enormous speed of the digital computer* more than makes up for this.

What is decimal 3 in binary code?

Turn to **125**

from 122

The arithmetic unit *adds, subtracts*, etc., and indeed performs all the necessary arithmetic operations.

Although we have said that computers often use *binary code* (a language with just two symbols 0 and 1) and we humans use decimal code (symbols 0–9 inclusive) for numbers, there are many other codes that are actually in practical use. We shall only mention a few in this programme. For example,

Octal code	(symbols 0–7 inclusive)
Duodecimal code	(symbols 0–9 and *two* new ones—*a* and *b*, say)
and Hexadecimal code	(symbols 0–9 and *six* new ones—*a, b, c, d, e* and *f*, say)

Hexadecimal code is what would be used in arithmetic, one suspects, if human beings had 16 toes instead of 10.

What is decimal number 5 in hexadecimal code?

Turn to **123**

from 123

3 is 11 in binary code.

We would like you now to remember that a computer has an *input*, a *storage system* (there may be different storage systems in any one computer) and an *output*.

Human beings have inputs through their eyes, ears and the senses of touch, taste and smell. Their brain is their storage system, and their output is their voice, and their hands and legs, in the main.

The computer frequently has paper tape and/or card input, many different types of electronic and magnetic store, and paper tape and/or card, or directly printed output mainly.

Although extremely fast at arithmetic, the computer is much slower at "reading in" and "writing out" information. Even so, it can do so very quickly indeed.

How many symbols need to be represented in the use of binary code?

Go to **126**

from 125

Two symbols only (usually 0 and 1) have to be used in binary code. This is precisely why it is so convenient.

In an octal code, how many *different* symbols are used?

129. Eight different symbols.
131. Ten different symbols.
135. Twelve different symbols.

from 134/137

True is the correct answer.

Decimal numbers can be both whole numbers and fractions. However, when you look at 0.34 or 26, you cannot tell just by looking whether they are decimal or not. They might be in any code which uses the digits from 0 to 6. This is easiest to see when you remember that a number like 101 could be binary, or it could be decimal (what we call "one hundred and one").

Now is the following statement true or false? "846 is an octal number."

133. False.
136. True.
139. I do not know.

from 133

No. 0, 1, 2, 3, which is your answer, makes up a *quadrary* system with just four symbols.

This would represent the decimal number 4 by the combination 10.

But it is the wrong answer to our question, so return to **133** and choose another answer.

from 126

Correct. An octal code is an eight-symbol code, and the obvious symbols to use are 0, 1, 2, . . . , 7, inclusive.

We should recognize next that all codes are compiled in much the same way. So binary is like decimal or any other code, in the way it is compiled.

Why is binary code so often used in digital computers?

Turn to **130**

130

from 129

Binary code is often used in computers because it needs only *two-state* switches to represent binary digits.

We have already talked about *coding*. We have especially emphasized that instructions and numbers have to be put into binary code for the computer to handle them, so we must consider how codes such as *binary codes* are constructed.

First, though, we must take another look at the ordinary *decimal code* of our everyday arithmetic.

How many different symbols occur in decimal code?

Go to **137**

131

from 126

No.

A decimal code has ten different symbols, not an octal code.

Return to **126**

from 133

You are quite right. Quinary systems use 0, 1, 2, 3, 4.

In the same way a decimal system uses 0, 1, 2, 3, 4, 5, 6, 7, 8, 9. An octal system uses 0, 1, 2, 3, 4, 5, 6, 7.

Now our special interest lies in the binary system, which uses 0 and 1 *only*.

Do not forget a *binary code* is similar to a decimal code, in that it is compiled in the same way, but with only two symbols. The numbers in ascending order are

0, 1, 10, 11, 100, 101, 110, 111, 1000, 1001, and so on.

These are the decimal numbers 0, 1, 2, 3, 4, 5, 6, 7, 8, 9 in binary code. We have not got a symbol 2 in binary code, so we must combine 1 and 0 to make an equivalent symbol for 2. 1 and 1 for 3, and so on.

Turn to **138**

133

from 127/136/139

846 is not an octal number and the reason is that an octal system has only the symbols 0, 1, 2, 3, 4, 5, 6, 7 and the number you were asked about contained the symbol 8.

Do not forget these number systems always start at 0. A *ternary* system, therefore, has just three symbols 0, 1, 2.

What symbols would you say occur in a *quinary* system of numbers? This is a system of numbers with five symbols.

128. 0, 1, 2, 3.
132. 0, 1, 2, 3, 4.
140. 1, 2, 3, 4, 5.

134

from 137

No, the statement that decimal numbers can be both whole numbers and fractions is true.

Both 26 and 0.34 are decimal numbers as far as we can tell. They might, of course, be part of a duodecimal code (a code having twelve symbols) and in which the two extra symbols do not appear. In the same way, 11 could be either a binary or a decimal number.

Go to **127**

135

from 126

Twelve different symbols are used in a duodecimal code, not in an octal code.

Go back to **126**

136

from 127

True, you say; but it is false, since an octal system of numbers has only the symbols 0, 1, 2, 3, 4, 5, 6 and 7.

It simply does not include the symbol 8.

Turn to **133**

from 130

Ten different symbols occur in decimal code. The symbols are 0–9 inclusive.

The decimal notation we normally use in arithmetic is *positional*, in that 12 really means 10 + 2, and 276 really means 200 + 70 + 6.

We "move to the left" one place after we have a number bigger than 9, another place to the left after 99, and so on.

Notice that numbers like 0.34 and 26 are *both* decimal numbers. It is important not to confuse decimal fractions with decimal numbers.

Decimal numbers can be both whole numbers and fractions.

Is this last statement true or false?

127. True.
134. False.

from 132

Binary	Decimal	Binary	Decimal
0	0	1000	8
1	1	1001	9
10	2	1010	10
11	3	1011	11
100	4	1100	12
101	5	1101	13
110	6	1110	14
111	7	1111	15

The binary code is generated by expressing a number in terms of powers of 2. For example, 15 is

$$(1 \times 2^3) + (1 \times 2^2) + (1 \times 2) + 1$$

which is in binary 1111.

A difficult question next. What is the decimal number 12 in duodecimal code (this is a code which uses twelve symbols)?

141. 12.
145. 10.
147. 11.
150. It needs a new symbol to say.

from 127

An octal code is constructed from a system of symbols 0, 1, 2, 3, 4, 5, 6 and 7. We can translate ordinary decimal numbers into octal quite simply.

Octal		Decimal	Octal		Decimal
0	=	0	4	=	4
1	=	1	5	=	5
2	=	2	6	=	6
3	=	3	7	=	7

Since there is no symbol 8 in octal, we continue:

Octal		Decimal
10	=	8
11	=	9
12	=	10
13	=	11 and so on.

The symbols 8 and 9 do not occur in octal, and this is why we combine 0's and 1's to represent 8 and 9.

Turn to **133**

140

from 133

The symbols 1, 2, 3, 4, 5 do make up a *quinary* system, and we will give you half marks if you like; but the trouble is that a quinary system of numbers starts at 0.

All number systems are to be thought of as starting at 0.

Return to **133**

141

from 138

In fact 12 in duodecimal code is 14 in decimal code, so you are wrong.

It is easy to get confused when you meet these problems for the first time so do not worry. Just return to the previous frame and think for a bit—use pencil and paper and try again. There is a real point in becoming familiar with the mode of construction of these numerical codes.

Go back to **138**

from 146

No. 010 is 2 in binary code.

The reason is that it can be written out $(0 \times 2^2) + (1 \times 2) + (0 \times 1)$.

Note that our little dodge of "moving to the left" involves multiplying by the *base* to some power. The base of a number system is the number of different digits in the system, e.g. binary is 2, decimal is 10. One move to the left means multiply by base (2 here) to the power of 1. Two moves means 2 to the power of 2 (2^2) and so on.

Note the phrase "to the power of" means the *index* or number of times the base is multiplied by itself, e.g. $10^3 = 10 \times 10 \times 10$.

Return to **146**

from 149/151

The binary number 101101 is made up of 32 + 8 + 4 + 1 which is 45.

Note that we say that the digit on the extreme left is the *most significant digit* and the one on the extreme right is the *least significant digit.*

This is another way of looking at it:

$$\begin{array}{r l}
2)\underline{45} & \\
2)\underline{22} & +1 \uparrow \\
2)\underline{11} & +0 \\
2)\underline{\ 5} & +1 \\
2)\underline{\ 2} & +1 \\
1 & +0 \\
\longrightarrow &
\end{array}$$

and this gives us 101101 if we follow the direction of the arrows.

What is the decimal equivalent of 10010?

Turn to **152**

from 146

100 in binary code, is equivalent to 4 in decimal code, so you will have to try again.

100 is short for $(1 \times 2^2) + (0 \times 2) + (0 \times 1)$. Note that our little dodge of "moving to the left" involves multiplying by the *base* to some power. One move to the left means multiply by base (2 here) to the power of 1. Two moves means 2 to the power of 2 (2^2) and so on.

Note that the phrase "to the power of" means the *index* or number of times the base is multiplied by itself. For example, $10^4 = 10 \times 10 \times 10 \times 10$.

Return to **146**

from 138

10 is quite right.

The duodecimal numbers, starting from 0 are 0, 1, 2, 3, 4, 5, 6, 7, 8, 9, *a*, *b*, 10, 11, 12, . . ., etc., because, of course, we use twelve basic symbols 0, 1, up to . . . up to what? We need two new symbols, so we shall use *a* and *b*, and that means that decimal 10 is duodecimal *a* and decimal 11 is duodecimal *b*, and now with decimal 12 we must start combining symbols and the first combination involves 0 and 1.

The difficulty is that we tend to think in terms of decimals. And the whole thing gets a little more difficult with fractions. 32.4 in decimal involves a decimal point. In duodecimal 23*b*.4 would involve a duodecimal point, and *binary* 01101.0110 involves a binary point.

What is duodecimal 1*a*.4 in decimal?

Go to **146**

from 145

1*a*.4 in duodecimal is 22.33 recurring in decimal. (Remember that decimal 0.4 means four-tenths, but duodecimal 0.4 means four-twelfths, that is, a third.)

Now let us remind ourselves of the following basic fact.

Computers normally use binary code, and all we ask is that you become roughly familiar with that.

Let us now test you on binary numbers. Which of the following binary numbers represents 3 in decimal code?

142. 010.
144. 100.
148. 10.
151. 011.

147

from 138

11 you say, but this is wrong.

11 is 11 in decimal, and in duodecimal it is the equivalent of 13 in decimal, so that should give you a hint.

Go back to **138**

from 146

No. 10 is the same as 010 since 0's to the left of 1's have no significance whatever.

This means that 10 is 2.

Go back to **146**

---

from 151

23 is your answer. But although you are wrong, you may merely have miscounted. The number was 101101.

And the first 1 on the extreme left (this is called the *most significant digit*, since it represents the largest number and is really 1×2^5), is 32; the next is 8; the next 1 is 4; and the last (*the least significant digit*, or 1×1) is 1, all of which adds up to 45.

Turn to **143** and see what is said to those who chose the correct answer.

from 138

It needs a new symbol according to you.

This is an idea, but a new symbol is unnecessary. The new symbols are those that stand for 10 and 11 in decimal and these are *a* and *b*, in duodecimal code; the new combinations of symbols never start with the end symbols but the beginning ones. So the next number is 10 as usual and does not have any connection with *a* and *b*.

We always start combining symbols with 1 and 0, and then 1 and 1, and so on.

Return to **138**

from 146

011. Quite correct. The 0 to the left has no significance, but the two 1's mean 2 and 1 respectively, so the total is 3.

The conversion, remember, from decimal numbers is a simple one:

> 0 = 0; 1 = 1; 10 = 2; 11 = 3; 100 = 4; 101 = 5;
> 110 = 6; 111 = 7; 1000 = 8; and so on.

The point is that we have to "move to the left" much more quickly in binary code because we only have the two symbols 0 and 1 to use. Thus 16 in decimal means only one "move to the left" and therefore has only two digits, whereas 16 in binary is 10000 involving four "moves to the left" and therefore has five digits.

Now write out the binary equivalents of the decimal numbers from 0 to 63, and then answer this question.

What is the decimal equivalent of the binary number 101101?

143. 45.
149. 23.
153. 44.

from 143

10010 is 18 in decimal.

To understand the general principle, consider again the following point:

254 in ordinary decimal numbers is really short for $(2 \times 10^2) + (5 \times 10) + (4 \times 1)$.

Now we need a little practice with the binary code so look at the following binary number:

11111.

Which of the following decimal numbers is the equivalent of it?

154. 32.
157. 31.
161. 33.

153

from 151

No.

Any binary number ending in 1 must be *odd*, so it could not, therefore, be the decimal equivalent of 44.

Go back to **151**

154

from 152

32 is *your* answer.

But you cannot be right, since you must see that if a 1 occurs at the extreme right-hand end (the least significant digit) the number must be an *odd* one.

Return to **152** and reconsider the problem

155

from 157

21100 is your answer.

And this is wrong, since the number "twenty-one thousand, one hundred" is:

$$(2 \times 10^4) + (1 \times 10^3) + (1 \times 10^2) + (0 \times 10) + (0 \times 1).$$

Go back to **157**

156

from 162

We asked you what the binary number 11101 looked like when written out in full. You chose $(1 \times 2^4) + (1 \times 2^3) + (1 \times 2^2) + (1 \times 2)$. But this is wrongly written.

$$\begin{array}{lr} (1 \times 2^4) \text{ gives } 16 = & 10000 \\ (1 \times 2^3) \text{ gives } \;\,8 = & 1000 \\ (1 \times 2^2) \text{ gives } \;\,4 = & 100 \\ (1 \times 2) \;\;\text{ gives } \;\,2 = & 10 \\ \hline & 11110 \\ \hline \end{array}$$

But the last digit of 11101 should be represented by (1×1) *not* (1×2).

Return to **162**

157

from 152/161

31 is the decimal equivalent of binary 11111.

The number is made up of $16 + 8 + 4 + 2 + 1$ and that is 31. Check it:

$$\begin{array}{r l}
2)\underline{31} & \\
2)\underline{15} & + 1 \uparrow \\
2)\underline{\ 7} & + 1 \\
2)\underline{\ 3} & + 1 \\
1 & + 1 \qquad \text{i.e. } 11111 \\
& \longrightarrow
\end{array}$$

Now look again at the general point: just as decimal 35 is $(3 \times 10) + 5$, binary 1101 is $(1 \times 2^3) + (1 \times 2^2) + (0 \times 2) + 1$ which is 13.

Now for practice, we must try this decimal number:

What is $(2 \times 10^4) + (1 \times 10^3) + (0 \times 10^2) + (0 \times 10) + 0$? Choose your answer:

155. 21100.
159. 10100.
162. 21000.
167. 2100.

from 160

19 in binary is certainly going to have a **1** at the extreme right-hand end (the least significant digit).

But 11001 is

	10000 =	16
	1000 =	8
and	1 =	1
	11001	25

We asked about 19, so return to **160.**

159

from 157

No, 10100 is not right.
The number ten thousand, one hundred is
$(1 \times 10^4) + (0 \times 10^3) + (1 \times 10^2) + (0 \times 10) + (0 \times 1)$.

Return to **157**

160

from 162

You are correct.
$(1 \times 2^4) + (1 \times 2^3) + (1 \times 2^2) + (0 \times 2) + (1 \times 1)$ is made up of

$$\begin{array}{r} 16 \\ +\ 8 \\ +\ 4 \\ +\ 1 \end{array}$$

and that makes 29 in decimals, or 11101 in binary.
Now, one more practice example: What is 19 in binary code?

158. 11001.
165. 10001.
168. 10011.

161

from 152

33 is your answer, and it is not correct.

It is certainly an odd number as the 1 in the extreme right-hand place (the least significant digit) suggests, but the value of the binary digits is 16, 8, 4, 2 and 1 and the sum of these is 31.

Go to **157**

from 157

Correct. 21000 (or "twenty-one thousand") is

$(2 \times 10^4) + (1 \times 10^3) + (0 \times 10^2) + (0 \times 10) + (0 \times 1)$.

It is a point to remember that, except for the symbol 2, you might have thought it a binary number, but the presence of a symbol 2 could never occur in a binary number.

Now you must not forget we are talking about binary numbers, and this is *the language of computers*; not always, of course, but more often than not.

What is the binary number 11101 written out in full?

156. $(1 \times 2^4) + (1 \times 2^3) + (1 \times 2^2) + (1 \times 2)$.
160. $(1 \times 2^4) + (1 \times 2^3) + (1 \times 2^2) + (0 \times 2) + (1 \times 1)$.
166. $(1 \times 2^4) + (1 \times 2^3) + (1 \times 2^2) + (1 \times 2) + (1 \times 1)$.

from 168

The most essential basic feature of a digital computer, we think, is that it has a stored programme of instructions.

This diagram pictures the basic relation between the store and the arithmetic unit:

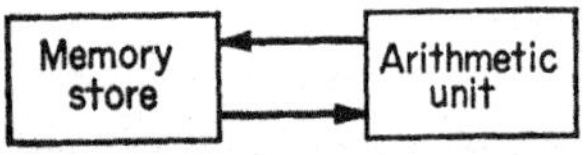

Let us suppose that we can gain access to any part of the store equally easily; . . . such a store is called a *random access store*.

Let us also assume the store will hold just 1000 words, and *words*, in "computer talk", mean almost any collection of symbols such as binary digits.

Which of the following may be computer words in computer (or machine) code?

169. 110011.
172. Shift one place to the left.
178. 1467.

from 169

We find computer words by their *address*.

We find the words we need in storage quite easily, *because each of them has an address*—just as human beings have addresses—and the address is usually a number, but not a road as well—a number is usually sufficient.

We shall assume the store of our very small computer has addresses which are composed of just three numerals or digits in decimal code; of course, for the computer they will be put into binary, but *we usually talk about them* for convenience in *ordinary decimal code*, to save space.

What is the total number of addresses that our small computer can carry?

170. 1000.
173. 8.

165

from 160

10001 is your answer. But this is 16 + 1 and that makes 17. Remember, in full, 10001 is

$$(1 \times 2^4) + (0 \times 2^3) + (0 \times 2^2) + (0 \times 2) + 1.$$

Return to **160** and try another answer.

166

from 162

You say

$$(1 \times 2^4) + (1 \times 2^3) + (1 \times 2^2) + 1(\times 2) + (1 \times 1)$$

is the same as 11101. But this is represented by 11111 in binary, and you were asked about 11101.

Return to **162**

from 157

2100 is $(2 \times 10^3) + (1 \times 10^2) + (0 \times 10 + 0)$
But this is not the number you were asked about, so you have made a mistake.

Return to **157** and try again.

---

from 160

10011, you say and that is right.

It is made up of 16 which is always the decimal equivalent to the fifth 1 to the left, and 2 and 1 which are the second and first 1's reading from right to left.

We shall suppose you have now acquired the general idea of binary code, even though you will need some more practice. Now let us go back to consider computers in general.

What would you say is the most essential basic feature of digital computers?

Turn to **163**

from 163

110011 is correct.

We have said that in machine (or computer) language any combination of *binary digits* is a word. In fact computers sometimes use other than binary codes, but we are going to keep to the binary code in this programme.

Now words are at least of two types—*instructions* and *numbers*. One tells the computer what to do and the other supplies the numbers on which the instructions operate.

Let us assume our computer holds eleven-digit words, ten digits for the number, with an extra digit for the *sign* (positive or negative, i.e. + or −), making eleven digits in all. Consider now the storage of these words, whether they be numbers or instructions.

How do we find computer words in the store?

Turn to **164**

from 164/173

1000 is correct, since more than 1000 would need to have four decimal places and we have only three available. We have the addresses 000 to 999 inclusive.

Just in case you have forgotten, the word "digit" means a symbol such as 0, 1, 2, 3, etc.

We say, for example, that the binary number 1001 has four binary digits, and this means simply the number of symbols making up the number. Actually, we would say that 1001 had four digits and uses two (different) symbols.

How many *different* symbols are used in the number 11210?

174. 5 (five).
179. 3 (three).

171

from 177/179

True is the correct answer.

The numbers 000 to 999 are the *addresses* of the instructions and the numbers in the computing store.

The control unit (C.U.) is made up of the instruction register (I.R.) and the sequence control register (S.C.R.).

When an address is passed into the S.C.R. 1 is added to the address, in preparation for calling up the next address, and meanwhile the I.R. obeys the instruction which it has just received.

If the S.C.R. had just received the address of the instruction in storage register 246, the next instruction to be acted upon would be—what?

175. 246.
180. 247.

from 163

Shift one place to the left.

This is a possible computer operation but it certainly is not a word *in computer language*.

Most computer words are binary words, and as far as we are concerned we can think of all words in the computer language as binary words, although we might *discuss them* here in decimal notation, or even use letters sometimes; but *for the computer itself*, they are always binary numbers.

So now, return to **163**, and we do not think you will have any doubt which is the right choice.

173

from 164

You say that a computer with addresses involving just 3 decimal places, has 8 different addresses.

If it were 3 binary places, you would be right, since then 111 would be the highest possible address, and you would have the right addresses 000 to 111 inclusive.

But we said 2 *decimal* places, so the answer is clearly 1000 numbered from 000 to 999.

Go to **170**

174

from 170

No. The number 11210 uses five digits, but only three of them are different, so we say *three* different symbols.

How many different symbols has 324 got?

Go to **179**

from 171/180

Yes, the S.C.R. "ticks up" 1, and *then* the instruction 246 is obeyed. Meanwhile S.C.R. has the address 247 in it, to call up 247 *after* 246 has been obeyed.

Now the instruction being obeyed may be an instruction such as "ADD the contents of 21 to the contents of 22 and place the result in 23".

This is what is performed by the control system informing the store of what changes to make. The actual process of addition is performed in the arithmetic unit and under the control of either the S.C.R. or the I.R.—which?

181. Sequence Control Register.
183. Instruction Register.

from 183

Decimal 13 is octal 15.

Decimal		Octal	Decimal		Octal
0	=	0	8	=	10
1	=	1	9	=	11
2	=	2	10	=	12
3	=	3	11	=	13
4	=	4	12	=	14
5	=	5	13	=	15
6	=	6	14	=	16
7	=	7	15	=	17

etc.

What is octal 15 when translated into binary code?

Turn to **182**

from 179

You are incorrect.

000 to 999 are the decimal numbers which are the *addresses* of the instructions and numbers in the high speed computing store.

Go to **171**

from 163

You say 1467.

This could be a computer word because we ourselves, *as programmers*, sometimes refer (using *programmer's language*, not the binary that is usually the *computer or machine language*) to computer words in decimal code, or even by letters of the alphabet, but we have said that *computer words* are always in binary, so we meant you to choose the binary number.

Return to **163** because you are wrong, and we want to remind you that computer words are in binary, even if we sometimes refer to them in decimal.

from 170/174

Three is correct.

Both 11210 and 324 have three *different* symbols. While a number like 010 has only two different symbols.

Now the addresses of our store are 000 to 999 in decimal code (programmer's language) and we shall say straight away that in most computers this would be the fast computer store. There would also be a much larger auxiliary (backing) store.

Now if we want to place instructions or numbers in store, we allocate a number from 000 to 999 to it. This is the *address* of the instruction or number.

Is the last statement true or false?

171. True.
177. False.

180

from 171

No. It is a slight trick really and not over important.

But we said in Chapter One, and we say again now, that the sequence control register counts up 1 from 246 to 247, where 247 is the address of the *next* instruction *to be called up*.

246 itself has still to be obeyed and is thus the *next* instruction to be acted on.

Go to **175**

181

from 175

No. If you guessed, you guessed wrong.

It is under the control of the instruction register (I.R.).

Turn to **183**

from 176

Octal 15 in binary code is 1101.

Remember octal 15 = decimal 13 = binary 1101.

This is all the practice we shall give on arithmetical codes, so proceed now to Chapter Four, which discusses the control unit in more detail, and some of the more general features of digital computers.

Turn to **184**

from 175/181

Instruction register is the correct answer.

Let us go back briefly to *codes*.

You can now distinguish the binary code used in most computers (the "computer language" or "machine language" as we call it) from the decimal code (the "programmer's language"). Of course, octal or duodecimal, or any other code, could be used for either language, but it is not a general practice.

The computer itself has, as we have said, the following general form:

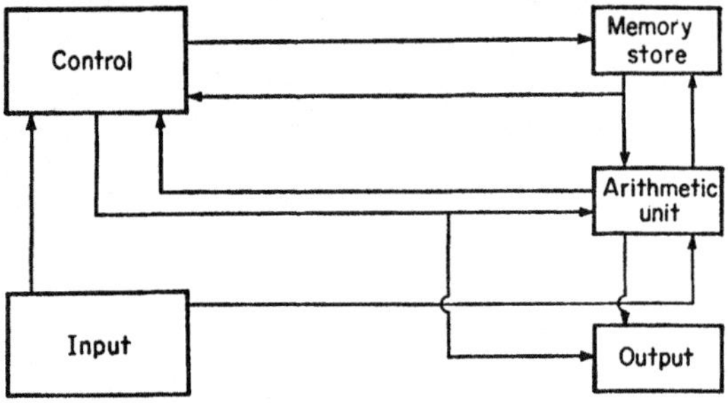

You should draw this diagram on a sheet of paper.

In the next chapter we shall take a closer look at the control unit and then design our own computer, called PRIMUS.

Another question on coding: What is decimal 13 in octal code?

Turn to **176**

from 182

CHAPTER FOUR

The Control Unit of the 3-Address Computer

WE SHALL explain in this chapter some of the more detailed workings of the *control unit.*

We shall also describe some more of the internal workings of PRIMUS, which is what we shall call our 3-*address computer.* At the same time, we shall take the opportunity to give revision and practice.

Look first of all now at our new block diagram which includes a more detailed picture of the mode of *control* of PRIMUS.

Go to **185**

from 184

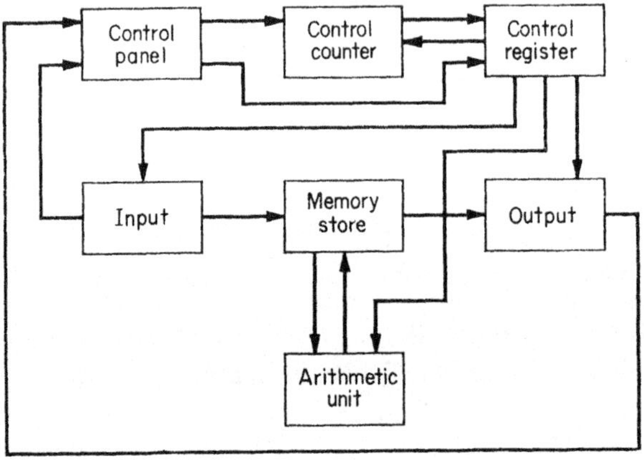

Note: the *function matrix* (that deciphers the function part of an instruction) and the power pack are not included in this diagram; furthermore, the computer and auxiliary stores are not distinguished in this diagram, as there is only one storage system in PRIMUS.

The auxiliary store is usually slow and large, and made as an extension of the computer store. We can forget the auxiliary store for all practical purposes.

Turn to 186

from 185

This fourth chapter is concerned first with a more detailed description of the control unit (C.U.) and its main constituents, the instruction register (I.R.) and the sequence control register (S.C.R.).

We shall start by describing a simple 3-address computer which we shall call PRIMUS, and we shall eventually describe its operation and *instruction code* in sufficient detail to allow us to programme it.

The operations it can perform are such things as *add* and *subtract*, and the instruction code simply tells us what symbols refer to these various operations.

A 3-address computer has the address of the two numbers to be operated on and the address of the register where the result is to be placed.

What is the general form of a 3-address computer word?

189. *F/A/B/C.*
197. *F/A/B.*

from 189

The three addresses in a 3-address computer refer to the contents of three registers containing:

(1) The number to be operated on.
(2) The number operating.
(3) The result of the operation.

Let us now construct an imaginary store:

000	001	002	003	004	....	009
010	011	012	013	014	....	019
020	021	022	023	024	....	029
:	:	:	:	:		
990	991	992	993	994	....	999

We can store a word in every position, each position is a separate register, and the number is the address of the register. Thus if the computer wants to read the word in address 013, it goes to the fourth column in row 01 and reads the word stored there. In this store there is room for . . . words.

Fill in the blank and turn to **190**

from 190

Instruction is right.

A computer distinguishes an instruction from a number by its location in store. So we have our instructions and numbers in store; we will worry later about how we got them there and, at the moment, we will say only that it is through the *input*. In the meantime we will consider the nature of the *instructions*, and the nature of the *numbers*.

You may recall that the general structure of our word in PRIMUS (using decimal digits) is $sx_0x_1x_2x_3x_4x_5x_6x_7x_8x_9$, where s stands for a sign digit.

Turn to **191**

from 186

F/A/B/C.

F means function, such as add, subtract, multiply, etc. The name "function" (or "operation") is sometimes used for the *F* part of an instruction word. So you are correct.

In a 3-address computer, what do the three addresses refer to?

Turn to **187**

from 187

1000 (we store the words in addresses, 000–999).

These stores may contain either number words or instruction words, and we shall suppose that *the first twenty rows* (*registers* 000–199) *contain instructions* (*or orders*) *and the rest* (200–999) *contain numbers* (*or data*).

Now what sort of word will occur in the storage location of our computer with address 008?

188. Instruction.
195. Number.

from 188

We could refer to the word as *sabcdefghij* instead of the way we have, but we then find it more difficult to identify the *position* of the digit. For example, is *h* the eighth letter in the alphabet? You have to count, but it is so. That is the problem, but we shall not worry about it, and *s*, by the way, means the *sign digit*, which tells us whether the number is positive (+) or negative (−).

Now we need an address number for each word and that we have already given.

Now test your memory.

Is 103 the address of an instruction or a number?

196. Number.
200. Instruction.

from 200

F/*A*/*B*/*C*.

Now the basic operation on a digital computer is the transfer of a number from one part of the computer to another. In a typical arithmetical operation one number is transferred to the arithmetic unit, and then it is followed by another number. Some definite arithmetical operation is then to be performed, such as adding the two numbers together. Of course, the instruction will tell us whether to *add*, to *subtract*, or whatever it is we have to do.

This means we have an instruction word which will be of the general form *F*/*A*/*B*/*C* (this is an instruction in a 3-address computer such as we are considering), where the letters *A*, *B* and *C* are the addresses, and the *F* is the name of the mathematical function or operation such as *add*, *subtract*, etc.

What does *C* in the instruction word *F*/*A*/*B*/*C* refer to in our 3-address computer?

Turn to **194**

from 198

02/200/201/202 means "subtract the contents of *201* from the contents of *200* and place the result in *202*", but this was not what you were asked to do.

Return to **198**

from 192

C is the address where the result (of performing *F* on *A* and *B*) is sent.

F/*A*/*B*/*C* is an instruction.

F means *function* (or operation), and the letters *A*, *B*, *C* are the addresses of the three numbers involved. If it is a matter of adding, then it is a question of adding the number in *B* to the number in *A*, and putting the result in *C*.

All the addresses are made up of three decimal digits and this leaves two decimal digits at the beginning (s and x_0 are the two digits) to supply the function.

If 01 is ADD, and the addresses to be used are 200, 201 and 202, what is the instruction to add the number in 201 to the number in 200, and place result in 202?

Turn to **198**

195

from 190

Number is your answer.

No. The first twenty rows, which make up the registers numbered 000 to 199, are for instructions, we said, and the rest take numbers.

So we must ask you to go back to **190** and have a careful look at the layout again, and then try the other answer.

196

from 191

But no, the first twenty rows from 00 to 19 are instructions, so instructions will always have addresses starting 00, 01, 02, 03, 000, etc. In fact the instructions are always placed in the addresses 000 to 199.

This means that numbers are stored in addresses where the first digit is taken between 2 and 9.

Go to **200**

from 186

The form *F*/*A*/*B* is that of a typical 2-address computer word. *F* is for function (or operation) and *A* and *B* are the two addresses of the numbers to be used.

Therefore you are wrong.

Return to **186**

from 194

01/200/201/202. (It means "ADD the number in 201 to the number in 200, and place the result in 202".)

We need a control unit in the computer to ensure that these instructions are carried out. It is made up mainly of an instruction register and a sequence control register (S.C.R.).

You can think of a register containing a number as simply a number written on a piece of paper and placed in a box, or a number on a mileage register in a car. These numbers, when they are instructions, have the function of controlling the transfer of the numbers from register to register, via the arithmetic unit.

Suppose our code for subtraction is 02; then what is the instruction word for subtracting 8 from 12, where 8 is in the register 200 and 12 is in 201, and the result is to go in 202?

193. 02/200/201/202.
203. 02/201/200/202.
207. We do not know enough to write the instruction.

from 203

The resultant of the instruction 01/200/204/208 goes in 208.

Now the C.U. includes, as we have said, the I.R., which deals with the instruction currently being followed (in fact "holds" the instruction which is currently being obeyed), and the S.C.R. simply counts, and adds 1 each time an instruction is obeyed, to bring up the next instruction to control, unless there is a change from the "natural order" in which instructions are accepted.

Now if instruction in 021 is being obeyed, and is in the instruction register, what will the address of the next instruction be, which appears in the S.C.R.

202. 022.
205. Any one at all.
211. 023.

200

from 191/196

Address 103 does contain an instruction.

Incidentally, we normally use capital letters A, B, . . ., N to refer to addresses without wishing to stipulate particular numbers. So we can talk of any three addresses as A, B and C.

If F is the function part of the instruction word, what is the general form of the instruction word?

Go to **192**

201

from 208/216

Correct.

The instructions are normally called up in sequence and adding 1 to the S.C.R. simply states the address of the next instruction which must be called up from store.

The sixth step is:

(6) *The control unit notifies the store to send the computer word, whose address is A, to the arithmetic unit.*

Where is A before this?

Go to **217**

from 199

Quite right.

It is easy enough; we just follow the numbers in the usual, or "natural", order of 1, 2, 3, . . . , etc.

Some computers can jump around and use instructions again and again in any sequence at all; but here we are following the general trend and letting instruction 021 follow 020, and this follows 019, and so on. Even in PRIMUS though, we may sometimes make *jumps*, but we shall leave that for now.

Now let us look even more carefully at the control unit. This sequences and organizes everything the computer does.

Consider the sequencing of the transfer of an instruction from the store to the C.U. This is fairly complicated, so you will do well to write the steps down, or draw a flow diagram of the operation. The first step is:

(1) *The sequence control register has the address of the next instruction to be obeyed, and the control unit alerts the computer to read this address.*

Now where will the instruction be sent?

206. Control unit.
209. Instruction register.
212. Sequence control register.

203

from 198

Correct. Do not forget in *F/A/B/C*, *A* is the "passive" and *B* the "active" address. We always operate on *A with B*.

Now back to stores for a moment. The name "temporary store" is used because instructions are usually transferred there from the permanent store before they are acted upon. The permanent store is also called the *auxiliary store*, and the temporary is often called *computer store*.

Where is the resultant placed as a result of the instruction 01/200/204/208?

Turn to **199**

204

from 209

011, you say. But 011 is the address and this would be in the S.C.R. The contents of 011 (the coded form of the instruction) would be in the I.R.

Return to **209** and before choosing the other answer, make sure you understand why this is correct.

from 199

Your answer, any one at all.

Well, we will not argue. There are some computers that are constructed that way, so you can dodge about as much as you like. But most computers, and that includes PRIMUS, are computers taking the instructions in sequential order, simply.

Therefore, after 021 comes 022 and so you should have chosen a different answer really.

Return to **199**

---

from 202

The control unit. Yes, in a way—half marks!

Of course, the instruction does come to the C.U. but to that part of it which is called the instruction register (I.R.).

You are not wholly wrong but we must ask you to go back to **202** and choose a better answer.

from 198

You do know enough.

8 is in 200, written 200(8), and we have 201(12) and 202 (result), and we know 02 is the code for subtraction. So reconsider the question before trying again.

Return to **198**

from 210

The I.R. contains the instruction currently being obeyed.
The fifth step is simply:

(5) *The control unit sends a message to the store to prepare it to read from the first address A which is in the instruction register.*

Now let us see if you are clear about this:

Why does the S.C.R. move up one at stage 3 of this (high speed) process of the computer?

219. To keep a count of the instructions used.
214. To bring the next instruction to I.R.
201. To prepare to bring in the next instruction.

from 202

The instruction register. Yes, indeed.

It is that part of the control unit called the instruction register which gets the next instruction.

And now notice a very important point. *This need not destroy the contents of the store,* since the instruction number can be simply copied out, leaving the original intact.

Now to the next step:

(2) *The control unit notifies the store to send the instruction to the instruction register* and this leads to step 3.

(3) *The control unit increases the sequence control register by* 1.

If the address of the instruction was 011, then what is now in the I.R.?

204. 011.

213. The contents of the register 011.

from 213

Sequence control register goes up by 1.

To remind you, so far we have the computer prepared to read the instruction from store; the store is told to send the instruction to the I.R. and at the same time the S.C.R. moves on 1.

What does the I.R. contain at any moment?

Turn to **208**

---

from 199

023 is your answer. It is not quite correct.

It is just that instructions do not go up in twos, as no doubt some things do; instructions go up in ones. The one way you could be right, though, would be if the instructions were taken in, more or less, any sequential order at all; they are in some machines—but not in ours.

Also, it is true that after 021 is obeyed, and before 022 is finished, 023 will be the address in the S.C.R. But that is not quite what was asked.

Return to **199**

from 202

The sequence control register.

No. The S.C.R. only contains the address of instruction that will follow the instruction being obeyed.

Return to **202**

from 209

Yes, it is the contents of 011.
Now the next step in the computer is:

(4) *The control unit sends a message to the arithmetic unit to expect the instruction which is now in the instruction register.* (This assumes that our instruction is one involving an arithmetic operation.)

The use of the word "expect" here means that the switches of the hardware (the word "hardware" means the actual physical parts like *valves*, *switches*, and the like) of the system have to be prepared to switch pulses from the I.R. to the arithmetic unit, in much the same way as we switch a train from one line to another.

What was step 3?

Turn to **210**

214

from 208/216

No.

The next instruction is brought to the I.R. by the C.U., but this is not the reason for increasing the S.C.R. by 1. The increase of the S.C.R. by 1, though, is vital to get the next instruction through correctly, since it is specifying the address of the next instruction.

Return to **208**

215

from 217

When an instruction is operated upon, the first step is to send A to the arithmetic unit (A.U.), then B follows, so we have $A + B$ in the A.U., if the function is to ADD; but we have not *yet* sent B to the A.U.

Go back to **217**

from 219

You were asked why the S.C.R. moves up one at stage 3 of the computer process, and your choice of answers is now reduced to:

214. To bring the next instruction into I.R.
201. To prepare to bring in the next instruction.

from 201

A is in the I.R. before it is sent to the A.U.
Now *A* is in the A.U.
And after this, the seventh step is:

(7) *The control unit notifies the store to read from B.*

What are the contents of the A.U. after step 7?

215. The contents of both *A* and *B*.
220. The contents of *A*.
225. Whatever was there before *plus A*.

from 220

Step No. 8 is:

(8) *The control unit notifies the store to send the word with address B to the arithmetic unit.*

Do not forget this may leave the original number in *B*, and just take a copy of it. It reads the word with address *B*.

Now what comes next?

224. The S.C.R. goes up by 1.
229. The C.U. notifies the store to send the word in *B* to the A.U.
231. The C.U. notifies the store to expect to read from *B*.
235. The C.U. notifies the A.U. to execute the function *F*.

from 208

No.

We can, of course, arrange to keep a count of the instructions used, and when we are taking the instructions in sequence, the number of the instruction tells us how far we have gone, but this is *NOT* the motive underlying this step.

Go to **216** and reconsider further this awkward point

from 217

Yes. You are quite right.

Every instruction word, in PRIMUS, contains three addresses since most instructions involve two numbers having an operation performed on them, and the resultant number must be given the third address. It is like saying "add the number in *B* to the number in *A* and put the result in *C*". The actual operation, which in our example was to ADD, is given by the first two digits of our eleven-digit word.

Right, now let us go back to our description of the computer control processing an instruction.

What is the next step?

Turn to **218**

221

from 235

You say the address of *C* is in *C*.

This is never the case. An address is the name of a register, and a register never contains its own address in this sort of computer, because instructions contain addresses, and these addresses always refer to numbers, and instructions and numbers in computer words are separated.

Try and remember what the computer has been doing in this rather complex process of controlling the operations inside the computer.

Return to **235**

222

from 232

Your answer, *A* is where the result goes. But you are wrong.

A and *B* supply the numbers that are to be operated on, and it is *C* that carries the answer.

Go to **236**

223

from 241

You say it is true.

But you are wrong, although it is perhaps a mean trick, because we have also said that the first 200 registers are devoted to *instructions* not to numbers.

Move on to **245** to see what was said to those who were correct first time.

224

from 218

No. We do not think you really mean it.

But in case you do, let us say that the S.C.R. goes up by 1 only when a complete instruction word has been obeyed, and when the last instruction has been sent to the I.R.

Return to **218**

225

from 217

The A.U. is cleared after each step, so that it will be empty when an instruction starts to be operated upon. This means that "whatever was there before" (i.e. in the A.U.) was nothing at all.

Return to **217**

from 236

The first step is "the sequence control register has the address of the next instruction to be obeyed, and the control unit alerts the computer to read the address".

The main thing that we have omitted so far from our description of the basic details of a digital computer is the input and output system, although there are also many other features of a computer with which one must become familiar.

Furthermore, there is the *console*, or *control panel*, which allows the human programmer to interrupt the activity of the computer, and this plays a very important part in the programming of digital computers.

The basic idea, though, is that use of instructions shall be automatic, and carried out by the 13 steps just outlined.

The most obvious omission from our discussion, so far, is *the range of possible instructions*.

We shall consider the *function code* or *operation code* (it is called both) for our small 1000 word computer, called PRIMUS.

Turn to **233**

from 235

C is in the I.R.

At the second step of the total operation the C.U. notified the store to send the instruction word to the I.R.

Now let us remember that this instruction word contains a function *F* and three addresses *A*, *B* and *C* of numbers. (The numbers in *A*, *B* and *C* can be referred to briefly as *a*, *b* and *c*.) So now to the next step.

(11) *The arithmetic unit notifies the control unit that the arithmetical step has been taken.*

This may last for a variable length of time according to the particular arithmetical step involved.

What would you expect to happen next at step 12? Think carefully and try to work it out before you turn to **232**.

from 232

You say we cannot yet know. You are wrong.

In fact from the start the idea was that the answer to the computation should be put in the storage register with address *C*.

Go to **236**

---

from 218

You say that the C.U. notifies the store to send the word in *B* to the A.U.

But this is not correct. This is exactly what we have just done in step 8, so it cannot be the *next* step.

We shall not hold this mistake against you, since we were only asking for an intelligent guess. But the right answer clearly must be one of the others.

Go back to **218** and try to work it out.

from 235

Your answer, the address *C* is in the A.U.

The address of a number or an instruction is not normally in the A.U. The A.U. contains only the actual numbers on which arithmetical operations are made.

Return to **235**

from 218

You say that the next step is that the C.U. notifies the store to expect to read from *B*. You are wrong.

This is already done at step 7, so obviously it will not want to do that again until the next instruction word comes round.

In fact both the words involved initially (with addresses *A* and *B*) are already in the A.U.

So think again! What must happen next?

It is true we have not actually told you the information this time, and we shall *not* normally ask you questions about information you have not been given. Nevertheless, you should be able to reason out the answer.

Return to **218**

from 227

The twelfth step is:

(12) *The C.U. notifies the A.U. to send the result of the arithmetical computation to the store.*

To what address in the store is it sent?

222. *A.*
228. We cannot yet know.
236. *C.*

from 226

Now the first thing is to decide what we want our computer to do, and naturally this will determine what sort of "hardware" (valves, relays, etc.) we put into our A.U.

So let us make it ADD, SUBTRACT, MULTIPLY and DIVIDE.

It must be able to *jump*; this is conditional on reaching some particular result, and we are expecting to have to explain this later on in detail. But we can say now that we might jump, for example, after having performed a division so many times. This would give us an answer to a certain number of places.

Turn to **234**

from 233

This is the sort of result we have in mind. This is called a *conditional* jump. The other sort of jump is called *unconditional*, and does not depend on some conditions being fulfilled.

And, furthermore, we will construct it to LOAD, PRINT and STOP. It must be able to perform these operations as a reasonable minimum. The STOP instruction, at least, will not require much explanation.

Let us call the numbers in the machine *a*, *b*, . . ., *n*, and say that *a* is the number in *A*, *b* is the number in *B*, and so on.

So let us ask simply, where shall we find *d*?

239. Anywhere at all.
244. In *D*.

from 218

You are quite right.
The answer is that the next step is:

(9) *The control unit notifies the arithmetic unit to execute the function F.*

Let us hope you had it right first time.
Now to the next step.

(10) *The control unit notifies the store to prepare to read the result into address C (the third address of the instruction word).*

Where is the address *C* at this point?

221. It is in *C*.
227. It is in the I.R.
230. It is in the A.U.

from 222/228/232

C is the correct answer.

A and *B* supply the numbers that are to be operated on and *C* is the address of the answer.

Now to the last step of the computer operation on the instruction word, *when performing arithmetical operations.*

(13) *The control unit returns to step* 1 *and starts again, going through the thirteen steps.*

To summarize the whole operation: the computer brings up the numbers in *A* and *B*; increases S.C.R. by 1; multiplies or adds them (in accordance with the function); and puts the answer in *C*.

Of course, the operation varies in detail with different computers, but this description is, in a sense, typical.

The system we have been describing is for a 3-*address* computer: the other equally well-known computers are the 2-*address* computer and the 1-*address* computer, and for these, the order of operation requires some modifications in detail.

What was step 1 of the thirteen steps?

Turn to **226**

from 244

No.

You are only adding the first two numbers, and the third number c is the result of the addition.

Return to **244**

from 242

Your answer, 01/009/007/000 is the instruction for subtracting 7 from 9. You are wrong.

In the *first* place 01 is the function number for addition.

We will say no more.

Return to **242**

from 234

Anywhere at all, you say. The whole point of our notation is that a is in A, b is in B, c is in C, d is in D, etc. We must, of course, eventually make A, B, C, D, etc., into numbers, so we can identify exactly which registers we are using. Similarly a, b, c, d *are* numbers. We also let the small letter represent the number which is in the register with the equivalent capital letter.

So you are not correct.

Turn to **244**

---

from 244

You say add a to b and store the answer in c.

Not quite right. Your mistake is in confusing c with C.

If the above statement had this change in it, you would be quite right. However, in this case it is not right.

The small letters are the names of the numbers (0's and 1's in the computer, of course), and the big letters are the registers where the numbers are kept—the addresses if you like—and these are in binary numbers in the computer.

Return to **244**

from 242

You are right. You have to know *where* these numbers 7 and 9 are, i.e. you have to know their addresses.

Without that information you cannot possibly phrase a computer instruction. So, if we said 7 was in the register with address 008 and 9 in register with address 009, you would be able to phrase the instruction correctly.

Is that statement we have just made true or false?

223. True.
245. False.

from 244

Add *a* to *b* and the result is *c*, you say. And you are right. It is just like 2 and 3 make 5, or 3 and 7 make 10.

All right, try to remember that, in the same way as in algebra, we use letters like *a* and *A* to stand for a whole range of numbers; the first are numbers such as 1, 2, 3, etc. (in binary in the computer itself), and the next are addresses—the addresses of the numbers (also in binary in the computer).

Our second instruction in PRIMUS is SUBTRACT, or SUB for short. SUB/*A*/*B*/*C* or 02/*A*/*B*/*C* simply means "subtract *B* (*b*) from *A* (*a*) and the result is *c*, which is put into *C*".

Let us look at a numerical example this time.

What is the instruction for subtracting 7 from 9?

238. 01/009/007/000.
241. Cannot give the instruction without more information.
250. 02/009/007/000.

from 256

Unconditional is your answer.

"Unconditional" implies that the jump is made at some predetermined part of the programme, but we have said nothing yet about this sort of jump; the only jump we have been concerned with so far is *conditional jump.*

You are not correct.

Go to **247**

from 234/239

In *D* is correct. *c* is in *C*, *e* is in *E*, etc.

In time we must identify *D*, *E*, etc., by number, and, of course, *d*, *e*, etc., are numbers.

Now to our first instruction which is ADD.

Naturally, we shall add two numbers and then store the result in some register.

Let the symbols 01 to 08 represent the instructions ADD, SUB, MUL, DIV, JUM, LOD, PRI and STO respectively, and therefore 01 is ADD.

What does the instruction 01/*A*/*B*/*C* mean?

237. Add the number *a*, *b* and *c* together.
240. Add *a* and *b* together and store in *c*.
242. Add *a* and *b* together and the result is *c*.

from 223/241

False is the correct answer.

In PRIMUS the instructions go in registers 000 to 199, and the numbers in 200 to 999. So let us put 7 in 200 and 9 in 201, and let us say the result should go in 202, so that the instruction is 02/201/200/202.

Our third instruction is MUL for multiply, and for which we use the (decimal) code 03.

And our fourth instruction is DIV for divide, and here we use (decimal) code 04.

What are the codes for add and subtract?

Turn to **248**

from 248

We have just told you the meaning of the instructions 01, 02, 03 and 04, so what does the instruction 03/*A*/*B*/*C* mean?

249. ADD the number in *B* to the number in *A* and put the result in *C*.

253. SUBTRACT the number in *B* from the number in *A* and put the result in *C*.

256. MULTIPLY the number in *A* by the number in *B* and put the result in *C*.

247

from 243/256

Conditional is correct.

It is conditional on whether one number is greater than or equal to another number or not, e.g. we change to *C*, if *A* contains 4 and *B* contains 3, but not if they are the other way around.

Jumps play a vital part in computer programming.

Now 06 (LOD) is concerned with loading and can be exemplified by the instruction word 06/*A*/*B*/*C* and it means "*load is words* (*the number in A says how many words*) *from the input into the store, starting at address in B, and when loading X complete, change S.C.R. to number in C*".

Now a memory test:

What are the first four functions of PRIMUS?

251. ADD, SUBTRACT, MULTIPLY and DIVIDE.

254. ADD, SUBTRACT, MULTIPLY and JUMP.

248

from 245

Add is 01, subtract is 02.

The code for multiply is 03, and for divide is 04.

Go to **246**

249

from 246

You say ADD, but you are wrong in this.

Even though the rest of the explanation is right, ADD is coded by 01 and not 03.

Return to **246**

250

from 242

You say 02/009/007/000.

We will admit that this is reasonable, although wrong.

02 stands for subtraction, but we do not have the address for 9, 7 or for the result of subtracting 7 from 9.

The instruction must refer to the addresses and not their contents.

Return to **242**

from 247/254

ADD(01), SUBTRACT(02), MULTIPLY(03), DIVIDE(04) are functions with codes respectively.

PRI/*A*/*B*/*C* or 07/*A*/*B*/*C* means:

> "PRINT *out a words* (*address A contains a*) *starting at address B, and change S.C.R. to address C.*"

and STO/*A*/*B*/*C* or 08/*A*/*B*/*C* means "STOP altogether".

(We can, if necessary, make our STOP instruction more complicated, but we shall not do so at the moment.) So STO does not use *A*, *B* or *C*. You must be sure you can write down the functions and their codes (the function code) for PRIMUS.

What are functions 05, 06, 07 and 08?

255. JUM, LOD, STO, CND.

258. JUM, LOD, PRI, STO.

260. JUM, PRI, LOD, STO.

from 258

Rounding off is a very important process. It involves taking a number to a certain number of significant places.

For example, if we had the number 23.8669, we might say, "take this to the nearest four digits (or two decimal places)", and this would mean 23.87, since the two places lost are 69; if they had been 39, then we would have taken 23.86.

It is just a matter of making approximations. You could just *chop off* the digits that will not fit into your register, but it is better to round off and take the nearest approximation such as 3.9 is nearest to 4 (if we have only one digit to represent it) and 3.4 is 3 to the nearest whole number.

Is rounding off needed with any other numerical operations besides multiplication?

257. No.
261. Yes.

253

from 246

You say SUBTRACT. But although the rest of the explanation is accurate, this is not.

SUBTRACT is coded 02 and the instruction you were asked about contained 03.

Return to **246**

254

from 247

You say ADD, SUBTRACT, MULTIPLY and JUMP.

But although the first three are correct, the fourth is wrong—the fourth instruction is to DIVIDE.

Jump is the fifth instruction.

Go to **251**

from 251

Your answer, JUM, LOD, STO, CND. CND is *not* an instruction. The others are right.

Go back to **251**

from 246

Yes, it's easy enough, isn't it? 03/*A*/*B*/*C* means "multiply the number in register *A* by the number in register *B*, and put the result in register *C*."

Now for the rest of the instructions:

(5) JUM for jump, coded 05.
(6) LOD for load, coded 06.
(7) PRI for print, coded 07.
(8) STO for stop, coded 08.

Now first of all, 05/*A*/*B*/*C* means

> "*if the number in A is greater than or equal to the number in B, change the number stored in S.C.R. to C.*"

This means that subject to the *condition* that one number is greater than or equal to another, then we change the *ordinary sequence* of instructions and go to the instruction in *C*.

Is the proper name for this sort of jump *conditional* or *unconditional*?

247. Conditional.
243. Unconditional.

257

from 252

No, you say. You are wrong.

The answer is *yes*. If you add two numbers together, the result is often a number that needs rounding off: for example, 9 and 6 make 15; if you were restricted to 1 place, "rounding off" would be necessary, although the result would not be very valuable since the approximation would be very crude.

Turn to **261**

from 251

Quite right. JUM, LOD, PRI and STO are codes 05, 06, 07 and 08 respectively, and they mean jump, load, print and stop.

So now our miniature computer PRIMUS has a complete *instruction code*, for the time being anyway. We can now perform arithmetical operations, making choices (as exemplified by making conditional jumps), and so on.

But there are still some problems to be discussed in programming PRIMUS.

One is that if you multiply two ten-digit words together you can finish up with a twenty-digit word. This means that we might easily lose vital digits off our numbers which could ruin our computations. This calls for a process of approximation; one of these methods is called *rounding off*. In fact this means we can only compute to the nearest ten digits.

Go to **252**

from 261

This is almost the end of our last chapter which has been mainly concerned with the basic information necessary to the programming of PRIMUS. But you should know that although it is simple it is quite typical.

Before we actually finish the chapter, we must revise some of what we have learned so far.

What are the addresses of the instructions and numbers in PRIMUS?

Turn to **262**

260

from 251

Your answer is JUM, PRI, LOD and STO, and we have tricked you a bit.

They are the right set of instructions but in the wrong order. JUM is 05, PRI is 07, LOD is 06 and STO is 08.

Return to **251**

261

from 252/257

Rounding off certainly applies to other operations besides multiplication.

If you add a ten-digit number to another ten-digit number you might well get too big an answer. Consider a simple case of adding three-digit decimal numbers, e.g. 846 and 930; the result is 1776 which is four digits.

It is clear, of course, that the increase in the number of places is generally less for addition than multiplication. But on the other hand, it is important to remember that if decimal points are involved, then the rounding off process may be easy and perhaps unimportant.

Turn to **259**

from 259

PRIMUS has a single store and stores *instructions* (000–199) and *numbers* (200–999).

The instructions have eleven decimal digits:

$sx_0x_1x_2x_3x_4x_5x_6x_7x_8x_9$.

sx_0 gives the *function*, $x_1x_2x_3$ is A, $x_4x_5x_6$ is B and $x_7x_8x_9$ is C.

For example, A is just a name for the three digits $x_1x_2x_3$. This is the *address* of a number. So $x_1x_2x_3$ could be any three decimal digits in the range 000–999.

Is this true or false?

265. True.
269. False.

from 269

Correct. *s* is the *sign* digit and $x_0x_1x_2x_3x_4x_5x_6x_7x_8x_9$ are decimal digits.

Of course, there will have to be many more digits in the *binary coded computer* word. But we shall not bother with that now.

Before we can arrange for PRIMUS to control our sets of electronic pulses which will represent our instructions in side PRIMUS, we must convert them into binary code. Then they become words made up only of 1's and 0's.

What is *F* in the instruction word?

Go to **267**

264

from 270

No. We did not call them sx_1.
The function is the first two digits of the instruction word. What did we call them?

Return to **270**

265

from 262

No. The digits $x_1x_2x_3$ are the address of a number.

Numbers in PRIMUS can only come in the range of addresses 200–999 except in one case which we will mention later.

Go to **269**

from 269

False. The digits $x_0x_1x_2x_3x_4x_5x_6x_7x_8x_9$ are *decimal* digits, and not binary digits.

Before the numbers and instructions are actually punched on tape to be fed into the computer, they will have to be converted into binary code.

But now we are talking *programmer's* language and not *computer's* language.

Return to **269**

from 263

F means the "function" part of the instruction word, which can also be called operation.

Now to remind you of the way the control unit works.

Let us say we are using storage registers 200, 201 and 202 for our numbers. Our instruction is in 008, say.

The S.C.R. reads 008, so the C.U. receives the contents of 008 (an *instruction*) from store, and prepares the A.U. for receipt of the contents of 200 and then 201.

S.C.R. meanwhile adds 1 to its address for the next instruction, which means it reads 009 which is where the next instruction is stored.

Then contents of 200 and 201 arrive at A.U.

The arithmetic step is taken, and control notifies A.U. to send result to 202.

The part of the C.U. which is performing this control activity is the I.R.

What is kept in the S.C.R.?

Turn to **270**

from 270

No. We might well have, but we did not call them x_0x_1.

The reason the first digit (the extreme left digit) is called s, is because of the *number* word, not the instruction word. (s stands for the sign of the number.)

Now what are the two digits representing the function part of the instruction word?

Return to **270**

from 262/265

False is correct.

The digits $x_1x_2x_3$ must lie in the range 200–999 as $x_1x_2x_3$ is the address of a *number* and that is where numbers are stored in PRIMUS.

Now the eleven digits

$$sx_0x_1x_2x_3x_4x_5x_6x_7x_8x_9$$

can also represent a number as well as an instruction. If we reserve s for the sign digit, what is the largest number that PRIMUS can hold?

263. 9,999,999,999.
266. 1,111,111,111.

from 267

The S.C.R. keeps the address of the instruction to be obeyed next.

The function of the A.U. is decided entirely by the nature of the function part of the instruction word. This is part of the *instruction* word, and is represented by what digits?

264. sx_1.
268. x_0x_1.
273. sx_0.

---

from 273

The complete instruction word is $F/A/B/C$ or sx_0 followed by the nine digits of the three addresses.

Finally, to complete our description of PRIMUS, apart from saying much as yet about its input and output (you can assume they are both in the form of punched cards), let us look at the *function code* or *operation code* of PRIMUS.

Go to **272**

from 271

The *function code* for PRIMUS is as follows:

Operation	Abbreviation	Programmer's code	Computer code
ADD	ADD	01	0001
SUBTRACT	SUB	02	0010
MULTIPLY	MUL	03	0011
DIVIDE	DIV	04	0100
JUMP	JUM	05	0101
LOAD	LOD	06	0110
PRINT	PRI	07	0111
STOP	STO	08	1000

You should copy this down for future reference.

Now turn to **274**

from 270

Quite right. sx_0 was the name we used.

sx_0 is the function or F part, of the *instruction word.* (However, in the *number word s* is the sign (+ or −) digit and x_0 is the *most* significant digit of the number itself.)

What makes up the rest of the instruction word?

Go to **271**

from 272

We have now told you the main features of a simple 3-address computer, PRIMUS. They are:

(1) It has an *input* which sends *words* into the computer.
(2) The words are of two kinds—*instruction words* and *number words*; both are given storage addresses.
(3) The control unit performs the necessary physical operations inside the computer.
(4) The address, the instructions and the numbers are all in binary code.
(5) The programmer must now organize the information so that numbers are passed to and from the arithmetic unit and operated on.
(6) The results are printed out.

You have now come to the end of this programme.

Index

OTHER LIBRARY TITLES OF INTEREST

F. H. GEORGE

Computer Arithmetic

K. C. PARTON

The Digital Computer

" . . . for executives and others in industry faced for the first time with using a computer, it should prove extremely useful." *British Communications and Electronics*

A. D. BOOTH

Digital Computers in Action

"The book, written in a refreshing style characteristic of Dean Booth, reflects his very wide knowledge of computers and their applications." *The British Computer Journal*

"The book provides valuable reading for anyone wishing to know what computers can do—and, to-day this should mean almost everyone." *Control*

D. WELBOURNE

Analogue Computing Methods